"Jason Clark is rapidly [illegible] r this present move of God arounc [illegible] rit-led worship leader and a powerful Spirit directed preacher and teacher, but he is also an accomplished Spirit filled word smith presenting Biblical truth in a powerful, unique and fun way. His keen and articulate incisiveness moves us to balanced thinking and foundational behavior.

It is not often my heart jumps when I read a book, but it did in reading *God Is (Not) In Control.* What incredible hope it releases, one that is biblically based and Holy Spirit witnessed to. What a vision Jason gives regarding our freedom as Christians, and how we must and can transition from control to love.

As you read and reread each chapter, as I have done, you will come to understand how you can be set free from the old teaching of sovereign control and begin to live in the fullness of all His Promises. This is a VERY NEEDED BOOK, WITH VERY NEEDED TRUTHS for the church today."

–RICHARD G OLIVER

Apostolic Overseer, The River Revival Fellowship, Pastor to Pastors, Speaker, & Author of, *Rich Oliver's Monday Morning Pep Talk*. Roseville CA.

"Jason is such a gift to the body of Christ. His intelligent, witty, and down-to-earth articulation of Kingdom truths invites readers from all walks of life to rethink troubling assumptions surrounding God's sovereignty. It's time the world better understood God's power through the non-coercive, freedom-creating, other-preferring life of Jesus. Jason's work invites the reader into this key theological journey!"

–JARED NEUSCH

Pastor, Bethel Church. Redding CA.

"Jason Clark, in my opinion, is one of the leading theological voices of our era. His fresh perspective comes from a genuine relationship with God. In seeking to know the Father, Son and Holy Spirit, we find ourselves, our meaning and our purpose. In *God Is (Not) In Control*, Jason encourages us in a more generous, increasingly life-giving understanding of the nature of God, and so points us in the direction of greater fruitfulness in our own lives. Thank you, Jason, for putting words to paper and making this book available to us all!"

–JENNY SHARKEY

Author of, *Christian Discipleship, Clinically Dead*, &, *A Glimpse of Eternity*, Founder, Jesus Hub. Auckland NZ.

"Like Jason's previous books, the goal behind this message is to remove any hindrance that might keep you from believing the truth of God's *always* good love.

Personally, the message of this book has been a wrecking ball to the long-standing theology of control in my life that undermined my access to trust, fearless faith and intimacy with God. I believe that while some may struggle with this books premise, there is reconcilable breakthrough, freedom, trust and deeper intimacy to be found in its pages. I believe this book will release you into life and earth transforming faith.

Thank you, Jason, for your obedience in writing this book."

–AARON ELLIOTT

Finance Director & Revenue Based Funding Investor. Charlotte NC.

"In *God Is (Not) In Control,* Jason Clark has opened up a floodgate of heartfelt revelation from our heavenly Father that will bring you into a greater understanding of His love. The work you hold in your hand is powerfully good and, at the same time, profoundly challenging.

This book is about a radical paradigm shift regarding one of the most divisive mental battlegrounds that the church faces, the question of pain. Questions like, "Why would God let this happen?" and, "What did we do to deserve this?" meet their match in this book. Quotes will be written down and pages will be annotated and worn from returning to them time and time again.

I fully anticipate this book will help an entire generation know the truth of the goodness our Father has in store for them."

–SAMUEL FARINATO

Pastoral Staff at Vertical Call. Santa Rosa, CA.

"Jason is a modern-day Caleb. He courageously explores unchartered territories and brings back exceptional fruit for us to taste. His new book, *God Is (Not) In Control,* is anything but comfortable. After all, he is reporting on giant-infested country, and sometimes he takes us close enough to smell their breath and see the color of their eyes. But he never loses sight of the one thing that enables us to hold our nerve: Our Father's always, always good love."

–PETE SCHELLER

Pastor, Destiny Christian Fellowship. Madison, WI.

"*God Is (Not) In Control* is a labor of love birthed out of Jason Clark's fervent desire to reveal God's goodness and expose the silent, but deadly theology that is the control narrative. By breaking down hefty matters of doctrine into smaller, chewable pieces, this book is a win for people of every background who are wrestling with the tension of the age-old question, 'If God is good, then why do bad things happen?'"

–CAROLINA PRECIADO
29-year-old Pastor & Church Planter. Charlotte NC.

"In his new book, *God Is (Not) In Control,* Jason challenges us to press into a deeper understanding of Gods Perfect Love. I believe this message and book will make a significant Kingdom impact by drawing people into an intimate relationship with their Father...maybe for the first time."

–BILL WOOLARD,
Owner & President, Third Day Capital, Inc.,
Wall Street Revealed, Inc. Charlotte, NC.

"Jason has written a beautiful book. While reading, I could hear the sound of freedom! *God Is (Not) In Control* reveals God's great and perfect love in a new way and is an invitation to change old paradigms and patterns of thinking. It is my prayer that this book will empower you and bring more freedom into your life."

–GERDA KEURENTJES
Speaker & Author of, *Heavenly Connection,* Senior Pastor,
Eldad Community. Ede, The Netherlands.

"My good friend Jason Clark has a true gift for being loved by God and for loving others; and he can't help but write about it. In his new book, *God Is (Not) In Control,* Jason has waded into a theological debate about the nature and character of God that has raged for centuries.

With the fresh and down to earth perspective of a practical theologian who cares about those who read his words more than his own ego or need for affirmation, Jason has written a book that will challenge your assumptions theologically and relationally with the profound truth that God's love is the core of His being."

–DR. JOSHUA FLETCHER
Missionary

"God is love and His love is always good is the message of Jason Clark's life. In his new book, *God Is (Not) in Control,* he helps us understand that sometimes, in order to grow in our relationship with a loving Father, we may need to step away from our boxed image of who God is.

You might feel uncomfortable, even tested by this message. But I believe Jason is the perfect author to guide you safely into deeper intimacy and trust. This is a book you will keep going back to in years to come."

–TRISHA FROST

Co-Founder, Shiloh Place Ministries, Co-Author of, *From Slavery to Sonship* &, *Unbound, Breaking Free of Life's Entanglements.* Myrtle Beach SC.

"Jason Clark invites us to challenge tradition and explore revelation. More importantly, he gives us the opportunity to upgrade our vision to the ultimate HD experience; seeing God as He is... 100% good, 100% of the time.

If your faith muscles have atrophied; this book is for you. If you want to know what it is to walk with God in an intimate way; this book is for you. As always, Jason delivers truth through a greater revelation of Love. My late dad would say, "let's take the 30,000-foot view." I believe *God Is (Not) In Control* is a 30,000-foot view the church is in need of."

–BETHANY SIGMON

Daughter, Wife, Entrepreneur, Loan Officer Assistant, & John 17 Advocate. Charlotte NC.

"Jason Clark gives us a new voice for grace and truth. He asks the necessary questions we often don't; and brings us the necessary answers we need. Highly recommended for all followers of the Lord Jesus Christ to grow in God."

–WILLIAM E. MOODY

Pastor, Valley Community Church, Teacher, Evangelist & fellow sojourner. Lima NY.

"The consummate storyteller, Jason Clark cuts through the theological mists and lays bare the core essence of God for all to see: that God is love and his love is always good. And that we can go beyond merely believing in this always-good God—we can revel in an uncomplicated relationship of intimate trust! Join the revelry...if you dare!"

–ROB EDWARDS

Pastor, Bayside Christian Church, Virginia Beach. VA.

"I grew up being taught that God was in control. It was how I understood His sovereignty. So, when bad things happened, God must have had a reason for either doing or allowing them in my life. However, Jason Clark's new book has goaded me along on my journey. It has shifted my paradigm from, *"God is in control"* to, *"God is always good and always loving."*

To be honest, I am going to be chewing on this book for a while. It has revealed truth that I believe will ultimately bring me into greater intimacy with my good and loving Father. Thank you, Jason, for pushing the envelope and challenging us to see Him more as He is and not as we have thought Him to be."

–MELINDA WILSON
M.A., Associate Director, Simply-Worship; Ordained with the River Revival Network. www.simply-worship.org. Sacramento CA.

""*"God is not in control."* I know, it's quite the declaration. Jason tackles this controversial claim while upholding the biblical truth of God's sovereignty. You see, these two things are not one in the same. Control is actually contrary to God's love.

So many people have written off a god they believe to be controlling and therefore unloving. But this book addresses that old belief system. It challenges you to think biblically instead of religiously. I'd encourage you to read this book from cover-to-cover and make a biblically sound conclusion of your own."

–CHRISTINE MCCALL ELLIOTT
Wife, Mother, Author, Pastor. Charlotte NC.

"Jesus said a lot of things that offended a lot of people, but wisdom calls us to look beneath the surface, to read between the lines, to open our hearts to the possibilities of who God really is, and He is not a controlling God. Proceed with an open mind and heart, question the things that need to be questioned, and allow Holy Spirit to influence your thinking.

God Is (Not) In Control kills some sacred cows, defeats some pride and frees your mind to allow your spirit man to be renewed. I pray this message releases freedom over your life and takes you deeper into the voice of the Lord."

–TERESA RICE
Writer. Charlotte NC.

"Deep inside these pages I found the statement I was looking for. It is a statement Jason made to me during one of our many lunches together. It was concerning the parable of the Prodigal Son--it arrested my attention, "*Another way to put it, control was not in the nature of the father, it was simply the perspective of an immature son.*" As he has so often done, in just one short sentence, Jason invited me to take a walk with him to view God from a perspective consistent with the narrative of sovereign love.

Jason has a unique handle on the revelation of the love of God. And this book is his invitation to explore that revelation with him. I have no doubt many statements will arrest your attention as well... but isn't that the nature of an encounter with love?"

–MARK APPLEYARD

Lead Pastor, Crossroads Church, Founder of Anothen,
Author of, *Think, Speak, Live - Business from Heaven's Perspective.* Charlotte NC.

"For many, the nature of God has been hijacked by a theology of control. But there is a Holy Spirit reformation today; sons and daughters are discovering a better perspective, a theology of love. *God Is (Not) In Control* is both important and beautiful beyond words. It opens eyes to see God for who He truly is. Jason writes in a way that empowers us to know God as unconditional Love in a world full of conditions. This book is sure to be both a seed and a turning point for many.

Thank you, Jason, for writing this!"

–PRESTON HALL

Director of Create58.com.

"If you've ever heard the statement, "God is in control" and it didn't sit right with you, there's a good reason. God is not in control, God IS Love. And my friend Jason Clark has written about it powerfully in His new book, *God Is (Not) In Control.* I was blown away by the revelation of God's goodness found in its pages. This is a book on the perfection of sovereign love. Do yourself a favor and read this book. I promise it will be worth it."

–CHRIS NAISH

I.T Network Engineer, Husband & Father. Martinsburg WV.

"*God Is (Not) In Control* is a faith-filled invitation to us Presbyterian and Reformed folks to see with the Spirit-enlightened eyes of our hearts. Our Reformation theology of God's sovereignty isn't about God controlling us or our circumstances, but about Father God loving us in all things.

Ephesians 4:4 says we are "chosen in love" and 1st John 4 tells us that God is love, His love abides in us, and His love casts out all fear of punishment. Jason vividly illustrates this by revealing that the Christian life isn't about a God who abides in us to control our bad behavior. No, the Christian life is about a sovereignly loving Father perfectly loving sons and daughters from the inside out and transforming our character. Let this book help open the eyes of your heart."

–DR. ALLEN V. KEMP

Former Co-Pastor, Suffern Presbyterian Church, Suffern, NY.
Presently, Father's Place of Rest. VA.

"From my relationship with Jason I have learned we share similar perspectives on the heart of God. Therefore, when I read *God Is (Not) In Control,* I expected a lot of head nodding acknowledgments that Jason's thoughts were similar to my own. And, while that definitely happened, approximately every few pages, I found Jason stepping on my toes!

I have been saying for quite a few years that Christians fear the freedoms of others and we often attempt to control their behavior so that we feel better. Jason's revelations about God and control revealed to me that I carry a little bit more of the control mindset than I cared to admit. Excellent book, eloquent and, as always, refreshing to read."

–DOUG CREW & SARAH CREW

President, Shiloh Place Ministries. Myrtle Beach SC.

"I am so excited about this book and it is an honor to endorse it! You see, the topic of God's sovereignty has been an ongoing conversation in my life and a point of wrestling in my personal prayer time. The message of *God Is (Not) In Control* has been a gracious invitation to discover God as sovereign Love. This fresh perspective has brought me to a point of peace. The book is so incredibly rich and well written. Regardless of where you fall on the issue, my invitation is to read it and ask God to speak to your heart. I believe He will."

–NATHANIEL VINKE

Lead Pastor, Fellowship Church. Clermont Ga.

"Jason is a dear friend, and excellent writer! This book disintegrates our man-made illusion of a hierarchical Sovereign, ruling from the cosmic distance, and using control to manipulate creation. He helps re-introduce us to the original Family from which we all came from, the Father, Son, and Holy Spirit. Driving the divine nail in the coffin of religion, Jason proclaims the nature of Their unconditional love, which is completely free from control. Dive in head first and drink in the news of a good God who is way better than anything you've ever possibly imagined!"

–TIM WRIGHT

Writer of, *Satisfied - Live at DreamHouse.*

"Hanging with my son, Jason, is one of the huge delights in my life. They are always unpretentious, authentic and serendipitous experiences. He usually drops what he's doing and gives me his undivided attention. Generosity, kindness and advocacy are the natural inclinations of his heart. I've never left our times together feeling beat up, confused, weirded out or discouraged.

I realize that most of you aren't going to get the chance to sit across the table, go hiking, or grab a coffee with Jason. But reading his stories about our good Father are the next best thing.

Jason believes to his core in the goodness of God. It emanates from his being. As you read his new book, the religiously skewed understanding of an intimidating, manipulating and dominating God will be replaced by an invite to an intimate relationship with Father God.

God Is (Not) In Control is an invitation to a friendship unlike any you've ever known or imagined. I pray you will walk away from this book with a full heart and hope swelling. Enjoy!!!"

–LLOYD CLARK

Pastoral Entrepreneur, Father, Husband, Friend & Jason's Dad. Charlotte NC.

OTHER BOOKS BY

JASON CLARK

PRONE TO LOVE

and

UNTAMED

GOD IS NOT IN CONTROL

(THE WHOLE STORY IS BETTER THAN YOU THINK)

A FAMILY STORY
18615 Coachman's Trace
Cornelius, NC 28031
Reach us on the internet: www.afamilystory.org

Cover Design by Nikki Hitchcock, SweetBirch Designs
Interior Design by Scottie A.B.

Funded and Produced by

BR

BookRally.com

Print ISBN: 978-1-946503-08-4
eBook ISBN: 978-1-946503-09-1

Printed in the United States.

DEDICATION

This book is dedicated to my family, the whole, beautiful lot. I am eternally grateful for your love, friendship, generosity and world changing faith…

…And to my wife, Karen, you are my absolute favorite and everything I have is yours. Love you. Love me.

ACKNOWLEDGEMENTS

Thank You, Father. Your friendship is my joy and salvation. May this book be a sweet, sweet sound to Your ears.

A book is never written alone. There are so many influencers – the dreamers and thinkers, the pioneers and reformers, the poets and revolutionaries, all who have prayed and believed, challenged, given, and loved so that this story could be told.

This book was not written alone. Every time I wrote, you all were with me…

Thank you to my family who has lived this message with me. Karen, your friendship and wisdom is stunning. Madeleine, my sunshine, Ethan, my wildman, Eva, my bright eyes - your love, friendship and trust is beautiful and world changing. I am amazed by you guys!

Thanks to my dad and mom. Your faith and love astounds me. Your friendship and wisdom is such a steady force. This book would not have been possible if you hadn't modeled a love that had nothing to do with control. I am eternally grateful.

To my father-and mother-in-law, J.V. and Cindy, for giving your daughter to a wild young revolutionary over 20 years ago and never letting on you were scared. Love you and your steady belief in God and in us.

To my sister, Aimee, and brother-in-law Eric, and my beautiful nieces, Sage and Lili. You guys are so authentic in love and good works; you believe like no one else I know. All of heaven cheers you on. I am eternally grateful for your love.

To my heroes, my brother Joel and sister-in-law Megan and awesome niece, Juno and nephew Elah. Dreaming and working with you, Joel, is one of my favorite things to do on the planet. And without your encouragement years ago, I would still be contemplating writing a book someday. And Megan, your grace and wisdom, to live as a catalyst to see lives transformed, astounds me. Love you both.

To my brother, Josiah. Thank you for your steady love and faith. Your generosity is stunning–love you. To my brother Benjamin, I have so loved travelling the world with you these last years. Your desire for God and adventure inspire me. Love your friendship.

To my sister-in-law Kathleen, and brother-in-law Aaron, and my incredible nieces and nephew, Taylor, Hunter and Gunner. Thank you for your friendship, love and encouragement. You guys are such giants in the faith and we love you lots!

Thanks to my brother-in-law's, Bobby and Martin. So grateful for your friendship and how you love us and the kids.

To those who have been such incredible friends to us, you have loved and encouraged, you have laid your lives down for us; Scott and Charissa Crowder. You guys dream with authority. Scott, your wisdom and friendship is life. Mark and Julie Appleyard, you guys live with promise so others can access theirs. Mark, I am truly honored to call you friend and blessed by your faith. To Jeff and Julie Watson, who believe and powerfully entrust. Joshua and Allison Fletcher, who love well. Aaron and Christine Elliott, who live as catalysts. Joe and Julie Jestus, who are trustworthy. Jeremy and Katheryn Cole, who are authentic in their love. Shannon and Michael Chambers, who live generous. Shawn and Brenda Ring, who believe for nations. Eric and Mary Vogen, who think higher. Stephen and Jane Prins, who encourage and live with grace. Joel and Tennille Carver, who live blessed and sure. Anthony and Mary Keith Skinner who live loved.

To my good friends who helped in the writing. Allen Arnold for letting me know I had a book in the mess of pages I sent a year ago. Thanks for your wisdom and friendship. To Nancy Bishay for your brilliant editing. This book is infinitely better because of your gift and grace. Nikki Hitchcock and SweetBirch Designs for the amazing and inspired cover. I'm so thankful for your generous encouragement. Thanks to Lexi Banales, Marcus Miller and everyone at Book Rally for helping me get this book across the finish line.

Thanks to everyone who supported the pre-purchase self-publish book campaign. Without you, this book wouldn't have been completed. I'm so grateful!

To our Newsong Church family, thanks for your generous transforming love and encouragement. So honored to run with you all. We love you guys! And our Crossroads Church family, thanks for loving us so well.

To my spiritual fathers and friends, some I know well, others from a distance. My dad, Lloyd, and mom, Mary Clark. Rich and Lindy Oliver, Bill Johnson, Dan Mohler, Graham Cooke, Danny Silk, Kris Vallotton, Dick Grout. You have no idea how grateful I am for the demonstration of your faith.

When I write, it is never without the company of melody and rhythm. Next to coffee, it is one of my favorite things about writing. Here's special mention of my favorite for this book, Seth Snider, The National, Alt-J, The Brilliance, M83, Bethel Music, Bon Iver, Eastern Conference Champions, Flagship, Hey Rosetta, Josh Baldwin, Jonathan and Melissa Helser, The Killers, Lord Huron, RY X, Neulore, Of Monsters and Men, Other Lives, Phosphorescent, The Moth & The Flame, Yes We Mystic, Foreign Air, Andy Squyres, Ten Fe', Mansionair, Foals, Ryan Adams, Hippo Campus, San Fermin, Anthony Skinner, Radiohead, Bleachers, Young The Giant, Wolfgang, Son Lux, The Tallest Man on Earth, Elbow, Kiev...

And thanks to my many barista friends.

CONTENTS

FOREWORD

BY DR. JONATHAN WELTON
BESTSELLING AUTHOR AND FOUNDER OF WELTON ACADEMY

The title of this book has possibly already scared off or offended some readers. Yet if you have opened it this far, my hope is that you will give Jason Clark a chance to rock your world.

God is in control is the type of assumed theology you would expect to find on bathroom wall placards. Rarely is it questioned, and not this directly.

But Jason is the kind of crazy that will take a newspaper and swat a Bulldog on the nose and expect the Bulldog to back down! And that is the kind of boldness needed to cook this sacred cow.

The concept of a God who controls everything is actually something that Christianity incorporated at the time of St. Augustine and it originated in the teachings of the pagan philosopher Plato. The concept greatly affects how we relate to God. But I encourage you to dig deeper and find out what the Bible says about how we relate to God? I believe you will find, like Jason suggests, that it's better than we think.

And this book will make you think.

If you are content to simply sit in a pew and have all your theology pre-chewed for you… then you probably won't like this book. This book is for the brave, the thinking, and those that want to have a closer more passionate relationship with God.

INTRODUCTION

BY SCOTT CROWDER
Singer/Songwriter & Senior Leader of DreamHouse Church
Newport News, VA. www.Jesusloves757.com

Love. Scholars and scientists, poets and priests, columnists and counselors, everyone has something to say about it. Shakespeare wrote nearly a million words, both comedy and tragedy. Love was always at the center. He once said, "Love is a terrible, wonderful thing." And all the people say, amen.

Why? Because we all have our baggage - our experiences and perceptions.

I remember being a kid and watching Tina Turner's music video, "What's Love Got to Do with It," on MTV. It was the early 80's. I didn't care for it. But I remember hearing my grandmother tell me how much she liked the song. I didn't get it at the time.

Years later I was able to put it together. That song released during a difficult season in my grandmother's life. She was going through a painful divorce from my grandfather. As the lyrics go, "who needs a heart when a heart can be broken?" Love had become a coded word, both sword and shield.

While this story is my grandmothers, we can all relate to the disappointment and insecurity she felt. We all have had an experience with love as the "terrible, wonderful thing." And yet, the whole world yearns to know love.

The Bible tells us that "God is love." That *should* settle our hearts. But because of our experiences and perceptions, many of us misunderstand *God's* love as a "terrible, wonderful thing."

And then, of course, we read Old Testament stories where God is associated with death and destruction and our insecurities and disappointments about His love are confirmed. While the whole world yearns for love, it's no wonder that many choose atheism or other gods.

But God so loved the world that He gave His Son… God reconciled us to Himself in Christ, He redeemed our experiences and perspectives. He revealed His love perfectly and then sent us the infilling revelation – Holy Spirit. And the fruit of His Spirit is love.

Love, joy, peace, patience, kindness, goodness, faithfulness, gentleness and self-control. *See Galatians 5:22-23*

Jason has stuck out his chin with the title, *God Is (Not) In Control.* He is willing to be misunderstood if that's what it takes for readers to experience the fruit of the Holy Spirit, a mature Christian faith. And Jason's risk is love's reward.

While the title may seem a strong statement, Jesus taught in similar ways, saying things like, *"If your eye causes you to sin pluck it out and throw it away." Matthew 5:29* I've yet to meet the one-eyed sin free man. But I have met so many who have been set free because they embraced the great truth hidden in Jesus' hyperbole.

For too long we have misunderstood God's love and power as control and abuse. Control is the perception and experience that has caused so many to keep God's love at arm's length. Control does not fit when describing God's love and this book sheds the bandages that bind and keep us from intimately knowing and trusting.

Love doesn't disgrace others. It isn't selfish. It doesn't fly off the handle in rage. It keeps no record of our mistakes. Love's delight is in rejoicing with the truth. Love protects and it always trusts, hopes and perseveres. Love never fails. *See 1st Corinthians 13:4-7*

I've heard Jason share this message in the church I lead. I've seen the transformation happen as hearts become whole. I've seen sons and daughters cry because they feel safe again in Daddy God's arms. God's love is good. You can be sure about that. And there is no control in His love. Love sets us free.

Readers - this is a great book. It will prove useful to many of you. I'm thankful Jason had the courage to write what I believe is a living work of reconciliation. Turn the page and open your heart to growing in love.

AUTHOR'S NOTE

This book is about *perspective* for the sake of *relationship.* While the subject is the sovereignty of God, this is not a theological textbook written to prove or defend some thought *about* God. I have simply written to reveal what I am discovering in my personal relationship *with* God. Yes, like all of us, I am a theologian. But I am not a systematic theologian with letters in front of his name, I am a relational theologian; a son, a husband, a father, a brother, a friend - I am loved and I love.

In this book, I have not written about Gods sovereignty through a rigid systematic lens. I have written through the lens of relationship. I don't approach God through disciplines, ethics and the dogma of religious thought; I approach God as an adored son of my Father, a beloved brother of Jesus, an intimate friend of Holy Spirit.

And it's all about family.

I am convinced family is the Kingdom Jesus talked about, the Kingdom He lived from, the Kingdom He revealed, the Kingdom He taught us to pray for and instructed us to establish here on earth as it is in heaven.

And you are a part of that family.

While I understand this books premise may cause many to feel tension, please know it's my great desire that every word reveals my love affair with Father, Son and Holy Spirit so that you might be encouraged in your own love affair. It's my great hope that you might grow deeper in a trusting intimate relationship with God.

Last, the sovereignty of God is an infinite revelation. I am but a child with a finite tongue. There is nothing I submit as absolutely definitive in this book except, God is love, His love is always good, and we exist to grow sure.

I pray this book encourages you to grow sure.

God Bless.

–JASON CLARK

chapter one

LADY LIBERTY

The Hidden Things

"I see it! It's a dolphin!"

My college roommate, Doug, was acting like he had just discovered a cure for Ebola.

"Sure, I see it too," I responded sarcastically. "It's riding a motorcycle while eating a hotdog."

"No, seriously!" he said. "It's a dolphin in the ocean. Can't you see it?"

Then another of my college friends exclaimed, "Mine is a pirate on a ship!"

He was standing just a few feet away looking at one of the other computer-generated pieces of "art" in the public gallery we were visiting that evening. There were twenty or so pieces on display in the room.

"This one is the Terminator!" a third friend announced with what seemed to be genuine wonder.

I thought they were messing with me, making it up. All I could see was a repetitive digital jumble of shapes and colors. Every poster size presentation looked like Max Headroom had attempted his best Jackson Pollock impression.

And much like a Jackson Pollock, each piece in this gallery was obscurely named. One mess of dots and triangles was titled *The Dolphin.* Another, *A Pirate on a Ship,* and then there was *Terminator.* The image that had captured my attention was apparently a *Unicorn and a Rainbow.*

I played along, “This unicorn is clearly representing humanity’s internal obsession with the illusion that is our external reality.”

Doug joined me in front of the piece. “You seriously can’t see it?” he asked, incredulous.

“Whatever,” I scoffed, but I was starting to think the fellas actually saw something I couldn’t see.

Then Doug, ever the helpful friend, patiently began to describe how there was a 3D image hidden in the repetitive design of neon squiggles and squares. He began to coach me.

“If you un-focus your eyes, the image will suddenly appear.”

I tried to ‘un-focus’, which isn’t even a word. It didn’t work.

Doug kept encouraging me while the other guys threw out random instructions between their outbursts of discovery. They seemed to see each new 3D image with greater ease.

“Squint your eyes… Wow, it’s a space ship flying over the moon.”

“Spin around, it helps if you’re dizzy... Cool, Darth Vader!”

“Just stare at your nose while keeping the picture in front of you… That doesn’t look like Pocahontas!”

I stood in front of that stupid picture of a unicorn and a rainbow for thirty minutes. Doug stood next to me, encouraging for at least another ten until he lost patience, "Just un-focus!"

"Un-focus? How does one do that?!" I thought, and also, "How do *you* know what Pocahontas looks like?"

The guys eventually moved on to whatever else that art gallery offered. I wouldn't know because I stood there, a stubborn, dizzy, cross-eyed idiot trying to will a mythical creature to magically appear.

Eventually the fellas got impatient, they were, *"leaving without you"* if I didn't join them at the car. I left dejected.

Over the next few years, 3D hidden art became an American experience. I couldn't go into a bookstore without one of those picture books mocking me for my apparent inability to see 3D images concealed within a sea of monotonous digital striations. Stupid unicorn.

Then one day at a Barnes and Noble, while my new bride Karen stood beside me, less and less-endearingly, exclaiming every ten seconds… "I see it, *A Bird on a Wire*", or "Oh, that one is fun, it's *Daffy Duck…*" I finally saw it! Revelation, at long last.

The image was titled *Lady Liberty*, and suddenly she exploded off the page in all her glorious wonder. Then, just as quickly, she was gone. Just dots and shapes again.

I didn't move. I willed myself calm. I waited.

"Come on out…" I coaxed in a whisper. I didn't want to spook her.

Then something began to shift; I could feel my eyes adjusting, seeing in a way they never had before.

"Easy now, careful…" I encouraged.

And then, there she was again. Clear and indisputable and brilliant! I wouldn't have been happier to see her if I had been an immigrant sailing in to Ellis Island for the first time.

I didn't take my eyes off the page. I didn't move. I wouldn't risk it lest my eyes reverted to their old way of seeing. I wasn't going to give her the opportunity to hide again. I stood in awe.

After some time, with a small measure of confidence and excitement building, I cautiously flipped to the next page. New neurons and synapses started firing; it was all there, The Dolphin, The Pirate, Darth Vader…

"He's right, that looks nothing like Pocahontas!"

I devoured picture after picture, then book after book, hidden 3D images materializing before my eyes, each quicker than the last. I couldn't see enough of them!

I had broken the code, reset my lens, shifted my perspective, I had entered a new paradigm, I was living in a new narrative, mysteries were being revealed, the hidden things were being made plain…

The Whole Story

Years ago, I stopped reading the whole Bible. You read correctly. For a period of about two years, I only read the gospels. Well, that's not fully true, occasionally I would brave my way into Psalms and Proverbs, but otherwise, I strictly and stubbornly stayed away from every book of the Bible except Matthew, Mark, Luke and John.

You see, I had discovered Lady Liberty in those pages and I wasn't going to take my eyes off her…

I love the Bible, the *whole* Bible. I believe the whole Bible is God inspired. He can be found in any and all of its pages. God has used the whole Bible to empower and instruct my faith from my beginning.

I remember my first picture Bible; I was five and so proud to have my very own. My dad read the *whole* book to me over the following months.

I still have my One Year Bible; I read the *whole* of it when I was 13.

When I was 18 I went to Bible College where I studied the *whole* Bible.

I love the whole Bible, and I continue to grow in my knowledge and love of it. But when I intentionally stopped reading the whole Bible for those two years, I did so for a reason. I had some unlearning to do.

Unlearning is a lot like un-focusing, except unlearning is actually a word.

Please understand...during those two years, I was not denying the whole Bible; I was resetting my lens. I had seen Lady Liberty. I had caught a glimpse of something hidden in plain sight. I could feel the eyes of my heart adjusting, seeing in a way they never had before. I couldn't afford to look away from the Gospels, the four books that are the clearest representation of Jesus, not even for a moment. I wouldn't risk it lest my eyes revert to their old way of seeing and I lost sight of the glorious revelation. I was seeing God like I never had before.

In Jesus, I discovered my core conviction, my whole theology - God is love, and His love is always good. It's that simple.

In those two years, I discovered that Jesus is the perfect revelation of what love looks like, acts like, sounds like, dreams like, teaches like...

Jesus is perfect theology - the clearest and truest way to know what God is like. He is the beginning, the end, and everything in between. He is everything before and everything after, measureless in love, infinitely good.

You see, most of my life I had developed whole thoughts about who God was by reading my whole Bible. By that, I mean, for too long I had allowed Job's or Noah's description of God to carry as much weight as Jesus'.

That's just dumb.

I am not suggesting God can't be discovered in the book of Job or in the story of Noah, but where the lives of Job and Noah are full of questions, Jesus is the answer.

And Jesus is the whole answer. Jesus is the whole truth. Jesus is the whole perfect revelation of God. Jesus is what the whole Bible is about. Jesus is what everything before points to and what everything after is built upon. Jesus is the whole story – His, yours and mine.

During those two years in the Gospels, I began to see Jesus more clearly. And I couldn't look away. Not for a second. He is wholly beautiful, wholly kind, wholly loving. During those two years when I didn't read the whole bible, Jesus was revealing the perfection of His love and He was making me whole.

I began seeing in a way I had never before. My old eyes, old thought patterns, and my old understanding of God were being renewed. I began seeing life in a new way. I discovered a better language, my native tongue. I discovered a truer paradigm, the Kingdom of heaven. The mysteries were being revealed; the hidden things were being made plain. God is love, His love is always good!

And my good and loving God looks like Jesus. And I fixed my eyes on Him and only Him as the *Author and Perfecter of my faith,*[1] as the whole story.

The revelation of Jesus as the whole story began shifting my perspective, my foundational approach to our relationship...to every relationship, actually. It changed my perspective on every circumstance; it also changed how I would eventually read the whole Bible.

Yes, I am again reading the whole Bible. But I read it differently now. Much like searching for the hidden image in 3D art, I look for the hidden revelation of Jesus, perfect love, in every page. And I am daily becoming better at finding Him.

Jesus is my lens. His narrative is my true narrative. His perfect love is my conviction. His goodness is my faith. Every question I have, every relationship or circumstance, every scripture, including the tension Job and Noah represent, is measured against the immeasurable revelation of Jesus.

Jesus is the whole gospel, the whole story. The perfect, unrestricted, all consuming, life transforming revelation of sovereign love.

---

[1]*Hebrews 12:2,* NASB

Two Narratives

I would like to suggest that there are two narratives on the planet, two ways to perceive in the world of man, two trees in the garden, two theologies by which to know God; control or love.

And I would like to suggest that we were born through Adam into a theology of control, but through the second Adam, through Christ, we can be born again.

The moment we said yes to Jesus, we were invited to transition from one narrative to another - from sinner to saint, from sorrow to joy, from mourning to dancing, from orphan to son, from lost to found, from law to grace, from slave to free, from a theology of control to a theology of love.

Before we were saved, we lived on earth as it is on earth. Upon surrendering our heart, soul, mind and strength to the perfect love of Jesus, we were invited to transition. We were invited to live *on earth as it is in heaven.*[2] We were given new eyes so we might see what was always there. We were invited into revelation; the active discovery of a love that is measureless, has no end, and is sovereign.

In this book, I am writing about our theology, our core thoughts about the nature of God, the lens by which we perceive Him. And in particular, I am writing about the vast difference between a theology of control and a theology of love.

Sovereign Love

Because He is God, Jesus is the best way to know what God is like. Jesus told us that if we have seen Him, we have seen the Father. He only said what He heard His Father say.[3] He only did what He saw His Father doing.[4] And the Spirit filled, led and empowered Him in everything He said and did.[5]

---

[2]*Matthew 6:10,* NIV
[3]*See John 14:9,* NIV
[4]*See John 5:19,* NIV
[5]*See Matthew 3:16, Matthew 4:1, & Luke 4:18,* NIV

I believe God is sovereign – *having supreme power or authority.*[6] And I believe any thought regarding the sovereignty of God that isn't found in the revelation of Jesus' life, death and resurrection should be held suspect.

If Jesus is the true and fullest picture of what God is like, then Jesus is also the true and fullest way to discover God's nature, His sovereignty.

And Jesus revealed God first and foremost as love. Everything Jesus did started and ended with love. God is love and He is always good. It says so in the Bible, the whole Bible, if you know how to look…

And Jesus, in His every breath, word and action, revealed this Love as complete, as the whole story, as sovereign. That's all in the whole Book as well. It just might require a little un-focusing to see it, a little unlearning to discover it…

Jesus was a perfect demonstration of God's sovereignty and He revealed it as Love.

Sovereign Love healed the sick, fed the hungry, and raised the dead. Sovereign Love forgave the prostitute, the adulterer, the thief, and the liar. Sovereign Love fed the hungry, cast out demons and calmed the storm. The power and authority of sovereign Love met and fully answered every fear and every need—physical, emotional, and spiritual.

Sovereign Love very much lived *on* earth, but He very much lived *from* heaven. And everywhere He went, the infinite narrative of Heaven, *love,* trumped the finite narrative on earth, *fear.* It always does.

But here is what's truly amazing to me, never once did sovereign Love establish the Kingdom of heaven on earth through acts of sovereign control.

While many of us believe the sovereignty of God has something to do with control, Jesus revealed the true definition of the sovereignty of God in the power and authority of sacrificial love; a love perfectly displayed in His life, death and resurrection.

---

[6]*Dictionary.com*

Jesus Never Controlled

Jesus, being fully God, perfectly revealed God's sovereignty. And Jesus spent His entire life revealing the sovereignty of God as love. A love with all authority, a love that was powerful and transformative, a love that forgave, and redeemed, and healed, and set free; love always sets us free.

And here is where it gets crazy good. Are you ready for this?

Jesus never once revealed God's sovereignty as controlling. Not once did sovereign Love force anyone to His will.

Jesus, the exact revelation of *supreme power and authority* on earth, never controlled anyone. Whether He was with the sinner or the faithful, the poor or the rich, His absolute power and authority was always revealed through love, not control.

Sovereign Love, in *supreme power and authority,* stood before the Sanhedrin and later Pontius Pilate, was whipped, beaten and hung on a cross, gave His life and died, and not once did He control another person.

This was not sovereignty as the world understood it. This was something altogether different and absolutely stunning; Jesus redefined sovereignty as perfect love.

And when He rose in majesty and beauty and wonder and saving grace, He demonstrated the ultimate *power and authority* of sovereign love. Even death couldn't hold Him down! Jesus put Death on notice. Nothing would ever be more powerful than perfect Love.

Jesus, in the mystery of fully man and fully God, deity in human form, and sovereignty perfectly revealed, lived on earth for thirty-three years and never once forced His will upon another. While He invited whole surrender, He never demanded, manipulated or coerced it. No one was ever compelled into servitude, browbeaten into following Him, or strong-armed into loving Him.

Jesus never once compromised free will. Please understand this, sovereign Love never once revealed, through His actions and words, a desire or interest in controlling us.

When I look at God through the revelation of Jesus, I don't see a God who seeks control. Quite the opposite, I see a God passionate about redeeming and empowering and setting free.

It bears repeating. Jesus is the best and truest way to discover God's sovereignty. He is the whole story. And He changed the lens, He broke the code, He revealed a new paradigm, a truer narrative. His sovereign love unveils the mysteries and makes the hidden things plain.

I Have to Tell You What I Have Seen

The revelation of Jesus as sovereign Love has changed the way I see and think about everything. It has been humbling and beautiful, powerful and freeing, and above all, transformative.

And it has been a little scary as well because it has led to writing a book on the sovereignty of God that goes against the last several centuries of popular Christian thinking. This book has been my most difficult to write because I am keenly aware that some may feel I am undermining or even challenging God's sovereignty - one of the very foundations of our faith.

And so, before going any further, I have written these next statements, I know to be true, in hopes to ease hearts.

I am fully convinced God is:

Omniscient; having complete or unlimited knowledge, awareness, or understanding; perceiving all things. *"His understanding is infinite."*[7]

Omnipresent; present everywhere at the same time. *"He is before all things and in Him all things hold together."*[8]

Omnipotent; almighty or infinite in power, as God. Having unlimited authority or power. *"For nothing will be impossible with God."*[9]

---

[7] *Psalms 147:5,* NASB
[8] *1st Colossians 1:17,* NIV
[9] *Luke 1:37,* ESV

I believe the Omni attributes of God are true. The question is, what story do they tell? Is it one of love or control?

I would like to suggest it can't be both and the whole story is better than you think. And this is what I hope to discover with you in the following pages.

You see, I absolutely believe God is sovereign, but as my hero friend Todd White says, "God is sovereign, and God is in control are two different thoughts, they are two totally different things…"

I have been growing sure in my native tongue, a language I was born again to rediscover. The language of love, and I must write!

My perspective is love and I'm seeing what was always there but I hadn't seen before. Like discovering the 3D image of Lady Liberty hidden in those pictures.

The more I focus on Jesus, the surer I am in the sovereignty of His love. I can see Him hidden in plain sight! And just as my mates in that art gallery all those years ago could not stay quiet, I have to tell you what I have seen.

And so, like my friend Doug, I am standing next to you humbly suggesting that you un-focus your eyes a little; suggesting that maybe, like me, you have lived in a world defined by sovereign control and there is a little unlearning to do. Maybe there is a greater revelation, a truer narrative in which to live, move and have our being.

Maybe Jesus is the perfect revelation of sovereignty. And maybe it's never been about control. At least, not the way we've always thought.

I invite you to journey with me as we navigate into the wonderful possibility that God is better than we think; that there is a greater revelation.

I invite you to see Lady Liberty realize before your very eyes!

chapter two

IT'S SIMPLE... GOD IS GOOD

If God Is Good...

If I type into Google's search bar, "If God is good..." Google will finish my search with the following suggestions.

...why is there suffering?

...why do bad things happen?

...why is there evil?

These questions reveal something sad and potentially devastating – most Google users – which is pretty much everyone on the planet – have a misunderstanding regarding the nature of God. The misunderstanding? They think God is in control...

In my early twenties, I had a conversation with a co-worker friend of mine who wanted to know about my faith. This girl didn't know Jesus; she hadn't experienced His always-good love, but she sincerely wanted to. So, I told her about Him.

I spoke with passion and power. I described a God who loves without reservation, a Lord who knows the number of hairs on her head and can be trusted with even the smallest of her needs, hurts and pains, a Father full of grace who desires to know her and to be known, a Friend that would never leave or forsake her, a Savior full of mercy and forgiveness who can redeem bad decisions and actions and every broken place, a Hope that never disappoints.

I described a good God who has loved her always and perfectly. Everything I said was true and we both could feel the power of God's goodness as I spoke.

She listened with rapt attention. She both wanted and needed to believe me; I could see it in her eyes and the tilt of her chin. Everything in her was crying out, "I want this love!"

Then she asked me *the* question. It's the question Google gets all the time; a question about God's sovereignty.

"If God is good, then why do bad things happen?"

She wasn't asking to be confrontational. She was sincere. It was clearly a question she had agonized over. It seemed to me she was desperate for a good answer.

I didn't know the answer. So, I gave her the answer most of us have given when we don't know the answer to a desperate question.

"God is in control," I said.

It's Simple...

For much of my life I believed God's sovereignty was defined by the simple and yet absolute idea of control. Because of that belief, I unknowingly complicated His goodness.

God is in control, simple. And that's where I put my faith.

God is good, true, but… well, it's complicated. I just need to have more faith in His sovereign control, and more faith, and more faith and…

And every time I placed more faith in sovereign control, His goodness became more complicated.

If God Is Good...

"If God is good, why do bad things happen?" she asked with life and death sincerity.

If I'd been truly honest, I was conflicted with the same question.

"I don't know, but He's good." That's what I wish I'd said, but I hadn't yet discovered that freedom.

Instead, feeling a sense of obligation, I responded the same way many well-intentioned Christians have over the last several centuries when faced with this very question. I gave her what I now believe to be a flawed statement regarding God's sovereignty.

"God is in control." I said. It rang hollow and powerless to our ears. So, I stumbled forward with the sledgehammer of a misunderstood scripture, "*…and He works all things together for good.*"[1]

Good, there's that word again.

"God is in control." This is the statement often used when we have no idea what else to say. For many it's a heartfelt declaration of faith when we don't understand, it's offered with the sincere intent to help someone through sorrow or loss or brokenness. It's the expression meant to encourage someone through disappointment. It's an attempt to describe the goodness of God so those who are suffering can be comforted. The heart behind this expression typically comes from a genuine desire to reveal the goodness of God.

The problem is, *"God is in control"* and *"God is good"* are two different and often vastly conflicting thoughts. And sorrow and disappointment expose the disparity between them like nothing else.

---

[1]*Romans 8:8*, Berean Literal Bible

My answer to her sincere question was meant to be comforting. It wasn't. However empathetic, it was an aspirin offered to a person with a life-threatening wound. It was anemic and ultimately destructive. Something wasn't lining up and we both knew it.

She looked utterly disappointed, a heavy weight crushing her soul. I watched her shift from hope, to deep sorrow and then rage.

"I can't trust a God who allows child abuse!" She said with agonizing force.

She described the darkest evil this world knows and I felt her confused and angry grief like a vicious slap across the face. My heart broke.

I think, somewhere in her life's journey, she had been a victim, she had experienced the devastating result of sin; the hell that exists in this fallen and broken world. And I had unwittingly told her that a good and loving God was the one responsible for her pain. My sincere attempt to share God's good love for her had only cemented her resistance to it.

"*God is in control*" was the only offering I knew to give her at the time. You see, while I believed that God was absolutely good, I also believed His sovereignty was inherently connected with the idea that He was in control of everything. Control was my theology; it was what I had been taught.

I subtly believed everything that happens, every event, natural, political, relational, every thought and intention, every dream and hope, loss and heartache, horror and death, disappointment and trial, were approved and endorsed by an absolutely good God in absolute control.

I also believed that control was the only way He could somehow work all things for good.

But there is a horrific problem with a theology of control. And it's pretty obvious. If God is in absolute control, He is also complicit in the horror of our broken experiences.

It's Simple...

My life, like yours, has had its share of sorrow, disappointment, and death; the evidence of living in this fallen broken world where sin has ravaged humanity.

For many years, even though I didn't realize it, most of my experiences where processed though my faith in a God who was sovereignly in control. With each tragedy or disappointment, I determined to make my understanding of His sovereign control *simpler* and thus my faith became more complicated, fragile and brittle.

The harder I tried to trust that God was in control of my fallen circumstance, the harder it was to trust His goodness and experience intimacy with Him in the midst of the circumstance.

As the years passed, my life became increasingly marked by fear, anxiety, disappointment, realism and such great insecurity. The more faith I placed in His sovereign control, the more His goodness became something to be experienced when I reached heaven. Eventually, the scripture I most identified with was the first half of Proverbs 13:12 *"Hope deferred makes the heart sick..."*

That portion of scripture said everything about my relationship with and faith in God.

And it makes sense. *"Faith is the substance of things hoped for"*[2] and my hope was fractured by the disparity of a God who was both absolutely in control and supposed to be always good.

Thankfully, God is truly and brilliantly, always good.

Over the many years of complicated faith, of trying harder, God faithfully led me time and again into His always-good love. He brought people convinced of His goodness into my life. He introduced books and messages that confirmed His goodness. And I pursued His goodness even though it was often in tension with what I believed about His sovereignty.

---

[2]*Hebrews 11:1,* KJV

Looking back, the transformative moments in my life, the moments where God met me through the Bible, prayer, or people, were always about discovering just how good and trustworthy His love is.

Looking back, I am amazed to realize that God never once asked me to believe He was in control, but He continually invited me to trust that He was good.

If you look back over your life, my guess is, you will discover the same thing…

Then, one beautiful sunny afternoon, God asked a beautifully *simple* question. It went something like this.

"Jason, is your faith in sovereign control or is your faith in My always-good love?"

If God Is Good…

If our theology is grounded in the idea that our good God is in control, then the Google questions make sense… Why *does* He allow evil, suffering and bad things?

It was my belief in sovereign control that led me to offer devastating rhetoric to my co-worker friend and use Scripture to compound the issue.

"He works all things together for good" loses much of its wonder and power when He is the one believed to have caused all the pain in the first place.

As though He is *"a good God who wants control of our lives and will partner with evil to get it; a good God who will compromise our freedom by manipulating evil circumstances to gain our affections; a good God who will allow love to be distorted and perverted to capitalize on our needs; a good God who is an accessory to murder, starvation, sickness, and poverty so that we would know He loves us,"*[3] a good God in sovereign control who would allow child abuse so He can work it all for good.

The contradiction is of epic proportions.

---

[3]*From Prone to Love*

It's Simple...

God is in control, that was my *simple*. But what if I made His goodness my *simple?*

What if I determined not to complicate things?

What if I put my faith in His always-good love instead of the idea of sovereign control? What would happen?

If God Is Good...

My co-worker friend had spoken truly; you *can't* trust a God who allows child abuse...

The idea that Gods sovereignty has anything to do with control paints Him as a needy bi-polar tyrant and positions humanity in the most hopeless and desperate of insecurities. The premise that God is in control manipulates His nature into something contrary to His always-good love and forces us into a *try harder* gospel.

It undermines our ability to trust and it complicates our faith. "*I just need to have more faith, and more faith, and more faith...*" but it's never enough.

A theology of sovereign control is like building your house on sand–the higher you go, the more unstable it becomes.

I would like to humbly suggest that God is either good, or He is in control, but He can't be both. And if we determine to make it both, we invite cracks into the very foundation of our faith.

It's Simple...

On that beautiful sunny afternoon when God asked, "Jason, is your faith in sovereign control, or in My always good love," I chose my *simple.*

God is love and His love is always good. Always.

Goodness is not a theory, or a concept; it's an absolute, a greater revelation of Jesus. When it comes to God, goodness is a truth we can either believe fully or not at all. God is fully, completely good, all the time. In embracing this truth, I have found the core value by which everything in my life is measured.

Life is about knowing His always-good love and then knowing more; it's about becoming sure. The gospel is *simple*; He loves us!

On that beautiful sunny afternoon, I determined to put my faith in simply believing His love is always good. And that simple faith began to un-complicate everything else.

If God Is Good...

If I could talk to my co-worker friend today, I would apologize for how I misrepresented Gods nature. I would challenge the controlling God premise. I would tell her that God is not about control; that sovereign love doesn't operate that way.

I would tell her that God has nothing to do with the evils of this world; or the devastation of sin. I would tell her He plays no part in hell or the destruction of humanity.

Then I would continue to tell her of the wonder of Jesus' love, a Love that *"works all things together for good."* Not because Love controls, but because Love is the most powerful revelation that exists, because Love has all authority and relentlessly redeems, always restores, and powerfully resurrects, because God's love is sovereign.

I would tell her that Love can be trusted because love is revealed perfectly in Jesus. I would tell her how Love trumps every disappointment, every evil, every control this world would seek to force upon us.

It's Simple...

I would like to suggest that God is asking you the same question?

"Is your faith in sovereign control, or in His sovereign, always-good love?"

I know many will want to choose both. I know this because I attempted it for much of my life. But if you attempt to choose both, the goodness of God will remain complicated and this complication will continue to undermine your faith. This complication will continue to position you in the desperation of insecurity. This complication will sabotage your confidence and subvert your hope. And most devastating, this complication will compromise your trust and undermine access to intimacy.

But what if you made His good love your *simple?* What if you put your faith there?

Maybe you would begin to grow surer in His affection, more confident in His love. Maybe your faith would become less complicated. Maybe you would discover a greater revelation of Jesus, Sovereign Love, the Tree of Life.

The second half of Proverbs 13:12 is "*...But desire fulfilled is a tree of life.*" That's the part of scripture we all long to identify with, the narrative we all yearn to live, the revelation by which we want to define our relationship with God. And Jesus revealed that it's meant to be!

"*...But desire fulfilled is a tree of life.*" That is the portion of scripture that I now choose to identify with. It says everything about my faith and relationship with God.

It's Simple, God Is Good

Many years ago, I decided that if I am ever unsure regarding something about God, it won't be regarding His always-good love.

It's simple, God is good. He is love and His love is perfect. Sovereign. And I have made it the compass by which I navigate life. My true north, my non-negotiable, my faith.

The controlling God premise behind the Google question "*if God is good*" is flawed and it complicates everything.

He. Is. Good.

And it's my heart's desire that we come to believe and know it so powerfully that the control narrative is changed; God is not defined by sovereign control; God is revealed through sovereign love.

chapter three

THE EARTH WAS NEVER FLAT

Once Upon a Time...

At the end of the 19th century the German pharmaceutical company, Bayer, prescribed "non-addictive" heroin for coughs. Around the same time, you could purchase Mrs. Winslow's Soothing Syrup to help ease your teething child's discomfort – it only contained 65 mgs of pure morphine.

Once upon a time there was a commonly held belief on the earth that heroin was good for coughs and morphine good for teething babies...

Circa. 570-495 B.C the ancient Greek philosopher Pythagoras proved the earth was a sphere, thus challenging a common misconception at the time that the earth was flat.

In 1543 Nicholas Copernicus debunked the commonly held belief that the earth was at the center of the universe. And in 1609 Galileo used the invention of the telescope to prove Copernicus correct, the earth revolved around the sun.

In 1917 Einstein's theory of a static universe was debunked by Edwin Hubble, inventor of the Hubble telescope. Edwin discovered the earth is actually ever expanding.

Once upon a time there was a commonly held belief that the earth was flat, at the center of the universe, and finite...

The Earth Isn't Flat

Imagine you've travelled back in time in your DeLorean time machine. You know, the car from the movie, Back to The Future.

There was Doc Brown, and terrorists, and plutonium and it was all very exciting. But you didn't go back to November 5, 1955...no, you traveled much further, way before the early breakthroughs in medicinal heroin and morphine, way before telescopes and Greek philosophers, all the way back to when the earth *was* flat.

You arrived in a field and, after sufficiently hiding your time machine, you began to explore your new surroundings. You came across two fellas at the edge of the sea in passionate debate. They were surrounded by a large crowd of people.

You joined the crowd just as the first guy points to the vast expanse of sea and beyond and says with great conviction, "10,000 miles, that's where the earth ends!" The other guy is adamant it's at least twice that distance. There seems to be support for both arguments from those in the crowd, heads nodding and fingers wagging.

Back and forth, the men debate with genuine spirit and intellect, each argument more impassioned than the last. And with each assertion those listening became more convinced.

You whisper playfully to a young man standing next to you, "What keeps us from falling off the edge?" The young man responds excitedly, "Elephants!" That makes you laugh so loud that one of the fella's takes notice.

He sees you standing there, in your Marty McFly vest, looking amused. You didn't mean to look amused, it's just, well, you have both pieced together the premise behind their debate, and, elephants?

"You! Yes, I am talking to you my strangely dressed newcomer friend. What do you believe; does the world end in 10,000 miles or 20?"

It's a tricky thing to be asked to settle a conflict in which both participants are arguing from a flawed premise; especially if it's a premise that all have agreed upon, a premise upon which, to some extent, their daily lives have been constructed.

But you, being a person who values truth, and, having actually seen photos of the earth in all its roundness, decide to tell them what you know. In a respectful tone, you say, "Ladies and gentlemen, you don't have the whole story, you're operating on a flawed assumption. You see, the earth isn't flat, it never has been, it just seems that way..."

It Just Seems That Way

Jesus found Himself in this figurative position.

Actually, many still believed the earth was flat when Jesus walked upon it, so, Jesus found Himself in this literal position as well. But He decided to leave the revelation of a round earth to Galileo and his friends. He had bigger fish to fry.

Sovereign control was introduced to humanity when it slithered into the Garden of Eden ages ago. It was the story told by Satan to the first Adam. And Adam bought it. He ate from the wrong tree. It distorted Adam's perspective on God, it imprisoned him to an inferior reality, a narrative of control; suddenly he was naked, ashamed and desperately afraid.

The lie of *sovereign control* birthed a world confined to human understanding; a world defined by human reasoning, "*a way that seems right to a man, but its end is the way to death.*"[1] And it produced a world ruled by fear, a perspective that led to finite flat earth conclusions.

---

[1]*Proverbs 14:12,* ESV

The devastating reality of this control narrative forced the first Adam out of the garden and into the wilderness where he passed the lie down the generations. It became intrinsic in every human experience, a violent reality on earth, a fractured lens through which humanity perceived, a mindset that dominated humankind, a paradigm of brokenness, a wilderness of human reasoning; the earth was flat and everyone agreed.

Except, as we know, the earth isn't flat, and it never has been. It just seems that way.

Then Jesus was born into this broken narrative, a world ruled completely by an ideology of sovereign control. And He revealed and redeemed a truer narrative. God was never about control. The earth was never flat, not even once.

Jesus, the second Adam, revealed powerfully the whole story, sovereign love. And in so doing, He exposed and declared war on the devastation of sovereign control.

The Devastation of Sovereign Control

"For God knows that when you eat from it your eyes will be opened, and you will be like God, knowing good and evil." Genesis 3:5

The ideology behind the lie Satan presented to Eve, and later Adam, was *God is in control.* And they bought it. They believed God was withholding some part of Himself. They believed some aspect of His nature was controlling. And by agreeing with this perversion of love, they enslaved humanity to the devastation of the control narrative.

Every horror in history, every fruit of sin, every sickness, every groaning of the earth, every insecurity, desperation and shame, every struggle "*against the spiritual forces of evil in the heavenly realms,*"[2] can be traced back to the moment Adam and Eve bought into the lie that the sovereignty of God had something to do with control.

Control… it's the very first lie the snake used to describe God. It exposed Adam and Eve's nakedness. It was the introduction of fear,

---

[2]*Ephesians 6:12,* NIV

condemnation and shame, the origin of sin and death, the birthplace of every religious thought and action thereafter.

Control…it masquerades in the religious rhetoric of holiness. Its wars are holy, its politics, its inquisitions, its crusades, its genocide, its prejudice, discrimination, racism, sexism, its abuse – all painted with the brush of fanatic righteousness.

Control…it's ego dressed up in virtue. It demands compliance; women must know their place, children must know their place, slaves, everyone must know their place.

Control…it's a bully who's been bullied. It's a vicious cycle of condemnation masquerading as justice. Its victims become disciples.

Control…it's the preacher frothing at the mouth about hell, and gays and gun rights. It's hate speech framed as pious obedience. It's the church standing up for what it's against while marginalizing all who Jesus embraced.

Control…it's the voice of social media mouthing off about tolerance while normalizing depravity. It's the doctrine of whatever feels good. It sexualizes everyone for its own amusement. It saves the whales while rationalizing abortion.

Control…it's the ethos of a fallen world, the lens through which most see, the context by which multitudes measure success, value, respect and significance. It promises we don't have to live afraid, desperate, helpless, exposed; that we don't have to be its victims. Except…

Control makes everyone its victim.

Deep down we know control is a mirage. We know it's a perversion of the truth; it's a counterfeit to the life we were designed for – to experience love and to become love. But to the extent we don't recognize or understand the power and authority of sovereign Love, is the extent to which we find ourselves clamoring for it: control of our God, control of our destinies, our jobs, our finances, our relationships, the line at Starbucks, the House, the Senate, the Mexican border, Russia.

Control is the lie driving a wedge into our relationship with God. It's a lie about God and a lie about us. If believed, it will demand to own our every breath, our every thought, our every moment. But it always leads to the same place – shame, condemnation, fear, death and slavery.

Control... it makes fearful slaves, and it never empowers sons or daughters.

Control... it's ugly, unkind and selfish. It's counter to all God is and yet it is still the word most often used to describe Him.

Control... we box God into a broken paradigm, a fallen narrative, a flawed premise, a lie spawned by the enemy of our soul, and then, when everything goes to hell, we, in our human reasoning, call it sovereignty and either blame Him for the brokenness or conclude He isn't as good or powerful as we thought.

This control narrative is an institution unto itself, a ruler by which human understanding has measured everything since the fall of the first Adam. The control narrative has dominated our thinking; it's become the pursuit of every religious, political and social institution on the planet, including the institution of Christianity.

A god in sovereign control is the devil's kingdom, and believing his lie leads us into the wilderness of our existence.

But it was never true; the earth was never flat, it just seems that way. Then, some two thousand years ago, the second Adam, Jesus, walked into this wilderness and declared war on the lie of sovereign control.

The Wilderness

Just before Jesus *"was led by the Spirit into the wilderness to be tempted by the devil,"*[3] His Father publically introduced the whole story.

"This is my Son, whom I love. With Him I am well pleased."[4]

"This is my son" - He is fully God and fully man. He is perfect.

[3]*Matthew 4:1,* NIV
[4]*Matthew 3:17,* NIV

"*Whom I love*" - He is living as the measureless revelation of sovereign love. He has all authority, the power of heaven at His back. He has come to destroy the control narrative.

"*With Him I am well pleased*" - He has all my pleasure; He is sure in my affection and He will establish my redeemed narrative on earth as it is in Heaven.

Then, Jesus, in the Father, led by and filled with the Holy Spirit, went into the wilderness to throw down the gauntlet.

You've seen the movie… two vast armies gathered, a valley between them. They are faced off against each other, ready to crush their enemy. But before a drop of blood spills, the leaders of both armies ride their horses into the valley to meet. Under a white flag, they look each other in the eye and make their demands. *"Surrender now and I will give you a position in my kingdom."*

We've all seen that movie. But this showdown in the Judean desert was different in two very significant ways. First, it took 40 days for Satan to get the nerve to show his face. Second, Jesus wasn't offering surrender.

Finally, punch-drunk by arrogance, Satan tries to capitalize on Jesus' physically weakened state. He attempts to persuade *sovereign Love* to submit to the devastating narrative of *sovereign control.*

Three times Satan essentially pleads, *"Acknowledge my control narrative and I'll put you in control of it. Endorse the devastation of my control paradigm and I'll give you my perversion of freedom by making you its dictator. Agree the earth is flat and I'll seat you over every pointless finite argument regarding where it ends."*

Control, is Satan's blindness. Control is the only narrative the devil knows, it's his theology, the only context by which he interacts with God and humanity. Therefore, he doesn't have the ability to comprehend the truth that sets free. You see, Satan's perversion of freedom is to be in control of others.

The fact is, that perverse perspective of freedom seeks to infiltrate every institution on the planet…

Because control is the only narrative Satan knows, he assumed Jesus came to earth to gain it. That's why, in the wilderness, he attempts to manipulate Jesus with promises of control. What he can't see is that Jesus came to expose the broken paradigm of control and reveal true freedom, the power and authority of sovereign love.

Jesus was fully man. He experienced all the emotions we feel. Physically weak and emotionally vulnerable, He was truly tempted in the wilderness. But Jesus was also fully God, and He knew the whole story.

Three times, Jesus essentially says, *"I am my Father's Son and there will be no quarter given, no clemency, no opportunity for surrender! I have come to destroy you and, along with you, the damning devastation of the control narrative!"*

Jesus made it clear, there would be no opportunity for retreat; the end of Satan's reign of fear through control was upon him.

At no time had the earth been flat!

Time Travel Continued…

Meanwhile, back to our time-travel voyage…

The fella that had asked for your thoughts seems intrigued. "What do you mean the earth isn't flat?"

Suddenly you're a little overwhelmed. You're not a scientist; you have no idea how to explain it (note - if you are a scientist, just ignore that last sentence… come to think on it, go ahead and ignore the next few as well).

"So, imagine the earth is like a big ball spinning on an axis, oh and it's in outer space." You pull out your smartphone so Google can help you make your point, but of course you have Sprint and there's no signal.

You're forced to use your words like you're a Baby-Boomer.

"So, this spinning ball, in outer space? Well, it's also orbiting around a bigger ball, the sun!" You point with confidence to the sun, hoping its existence will help prove your point.

"What keeps us from falling off?" One of the fellas asks quizzically. He seems uncomfortably intrigued.

The young man next to you asks hopefully, "Elephants?"

You are about to attempt an explanation of gravity when you are struck with two very valid concerns. First, you don't know how gravity works; second, you suddenly remember Doc's words, something about not *"unraveling the very fabric of the space-time continuum."*

The whole crowd is still waiting for an answer and it dawns on you that it's going to take way more than a vague memory of your 7th grade science class to convince them the earth isn't flat. It will require something of grand proportions, a greater revelation, to change their flat-earth thinking.

Sovereign Love

Having won the desert showdown, Jesus left the wilderness on a mission, *His face set like flint.*[5] He lived in our finite world controlled by measurements; a world dominated by fear, and He revealed a measureless, infinite perfect love that casts out all fear.[6]

He walked among the flat-earthers and revealed the whole story, sovereign love! Everywhere sovereign Love walked, the ugly lie of sovereign control was exposed and its power destroyed!

Sovereign Love destroyed every control; He healed blind eyes, cleansed lepers, fed the hungry, clothed the poor, raises the dead!

Sovereign Love decimated the destruction of a theology of control by setting captives free. He transformed, sinners to saints, and slaves

---

[5]*See Luke 9:51,* NIV; Isaiah 50:6-7, NIV
[6]*See 1 John 4:18,* NIV

to sons and daughters. He restored and redeemed the worst of life's tragedies and He healed the most broken of life's sorrows.

Then sovereign Love experienced the ultimate control, death. And He revealed sovereign love was more powerful than death by rising from the grave.

And upon His resurrection, He won our freedom, redeemed our narrative and gave us access to a His perspective - the earth wasn't flat.

Not only was a battle won, the war was won. Sovereign love was victorious!

How Does He Win in The End?

"If God is not in control, how does He win in the end? He has to be in control to win." My friend said this with a force that bordered panic. He was uncomfortable by what I had just suggested.

We sat in a local bakery, my coffee was cold; I hadn't taken a sip for fifteen minutes. I'd been sharing both about the devastation of *sovereign control* and the goodness of *sovereign love.* I concluded by suggesting that maybe *control* wasn't the best way to describe God.

"How do we win in the end?" I repeated, "What if that's the wrong question? What if the earth was never flat, it just seems that way?"

"What do you mean?" he asked understandably confused. I hadn't told him about our time travel adventures and the two fellas on the beach.

"What if the premise behind your question is wrong? What if believing God is in control is like believing the earth is flat? It seems right from our perspective. It seems a necessity if God is to win in the end. But what if there is another way to win, a better way. A way that doesn't complicate God's goodness or compromise His love?"

I could see my friend was still very uncomfortable. I shrugged and smiled, "It's just a thought."

I let it go. But I could have kept on.

What if the sovereignty of God wasn't about control, but was defined truly and perfectly through love? What if sovereign Love has already won because that's the nature of love? What if sovereign Love never loses, He simply redeems the past and transforms the future?

What if God was never in control; it just seems that way.

Then, what if Jesus did something of such grand proportions, something so powerful, that our flat-earth perception and thinking could be forever changed? What if He lived, died and rose so we could be free and empowered, so we could see and experience a truer paradigm, the whole story, sovereign love?

What if the very real war we are waging, a war that is evident in so many aspects of daily life, a war marked by disappointment and sorrow, sin and death, sickness, doubt and shame, is a war against the devastating lie of sovereign control.

And what if this war has already been won?

I would like to suggest that sovereign control is flat earth thinking, it's an institution unto itself, a broken paradigm, a ruler by which so many have measured everything since the fall of Adam. This devastating narrative has dominated humanity's thoughts and perceptions for far too long!

Jesus redeemed our true narrative, He redefined His sovereignty as perfect Love. He restored us to our original relationship before the fall, and He empowered trust and set us free so we could live confidently victorious.

The earth is not flat, it just seems that way.

chapter four

UNRAVELING THE UNIVERSE

Unraveling the Universe

Years ago, I was wrapping up final edits for my book, *Prone to Love*. I had sent the manuscript to a few close friends, pastors, authors and leaders whom I love and esteem. I requested both feedback and endorsements.

I highly value this part of the editing process. It gives me a chance to *see* what I've written from another's perspective and, in so doing, discover better ways to communicate. The editing insight I gain is priceless.

When it came to *Prone to Love*, one of my pastor friends was both alarmed and offended by a particular idea I had presented; an idea that challenged a common perception of God. I had written an entire chapter under the title, *"God Is Not In Control,"* and my friend was greatly unsettled by the thought.

To him, proposing the idea that God is not in control was the equivalent of "pulling a string that unravels the universe." That's what he said.

He implored me to make edits, informing me that if I didn't, not only would he decline endorsing the book; he would regrettably have to distance himself from me.

While I was surprised by how earnest he was in his disagreement, and by how distraught he was over my assertions, I was grateful for his feedback. I had one aspiration for *Prone to Love*—that my reader would discover how wide, and long, and high, and deep is our Father's always-good and transforming love.[1]

I had no desire to unnecessarily sidetrack the reader in the oft-heated debate regarding God's sovereignty. While it's clearly an important subject to me, I didn't want the message of *Prone to Love* to become hijacked by an avoidable offense. So, I made a very simple edit.

Everywhere I had written, *"God is not in control,"* I changed to *"God is not controlling."*

By slightly altering my approach, I hoped to subtly challenge what I believed to be a dysfunctional idea – the idea of sovereign control - without taking the reader down a rabbit trail we needn't have traveled at the time.

And it worked.

I sent the chapter back to my friend and he thanked me. He was "encouraged" and "relieved!"

And I was intrigued.

You see, I hadn't changed the content; the chapter pointed to the same truths and came to the same conclusions. The only difference was the way I'd navigated the word *control.*

My pastor friend seemed to be good with the idea that God is not controlling, just as long as He is still in control. I have found this to be

---

[1]*Ephesians 3:18,* NIV

the case with others as well.

Because God Is Sovereign

If someone introduced me as a good father, no one would interpret that to mean that I was a perfect father. That's because I am not the definition of a good father. I am not the standard bearer. You see, I am not sovereign; I am human.

But it's not that way with God. He is sovereign. He is infinite. He *is* the standard bearer. So, when we say, "God is a good Father," we are saying, "God is the perfect infinite representation of a good Father. He is the definition, the high-water mark of what a good Father is like."

You'll notice that even when writing about God, I delineate by capitalizing whenever I reference Him. Why, because God is sovereign, "*supreme in power and authority*."[2]

"God is light and there is no darkness in Him."[3] This verse in 1st John reveals how God, in His sovereignty, is the perfect definition of light. Therefore, we can conclude that every interaction with God will be illuminating.

Just so, when we read in 1st John that *"God is love,"*[4] what we are reading is that, God, in His sovereignty, perfectly defines love. Therefore, we can conclude that every interaction with God will be loving.

My point? If sovereign light is always sovereignly illuminating, and sovereign love is always sovereignly loving, then sovereign control would always be sovereignly controlling.

I would like to suggest that because God is sovereign, it's not possible for Him to be in control and not be controlling.

Control = Controlling

"Dad, is it OK to say God is in control of the weather and still believe that God is not controlling?" We were driving to Ethan's football practice when he asked this question. It was just the two of us.

---

[2]*See Dictionary.com*
[3]*1 John 1:5,* ESV
[4]*1 John 4:8,* NIV

The night before, my fourteen-year-old son had watched a teaching video with his youth group in which the presenter described the sovereignty of God the way I've most often heard it described, "*God was in control.*"

Ethan is a brilliant and thoughtful young man. He was good with the idea that God is not controlling. But he knew his dad was writing a book that follows that thought to an uncomfortable, unraveling and for many, unsettling conclusion.

"You could say that son. But implicit in that statement is a problematic conclusion. If we believe God is in control of the weather, then the moment anything happens with the weather, He is being controlling. It's all well and good when there's a gentle rain, but what do we do with a Tsunami?

What do we do when the flood from that Tsunami kills a person, or a hundred persons, or a thousand persons?"

Ethan saw the problem immediately.

The fact is, a God sovereignly in control of the weather sounds great until we take the thought to its conclusion. You see, a God in sovereign control of the weather, means God is sovereignly controlling the weather. Control is always evidenced through the act of controlling.

My point? A God in sovereign control, is a controlling God. And a controlling God places humanity in the most desperate of insecurity because a controlling God is culpable for the devastation of the tsunami.

A Gun Is a Gun

To suggest God is in control but isn't controlling is a little like saying, "God carries a gun but never uses it… or rarely uses it, or, well, you never know when He is going to use it."

Eventually it breaks down to, "God carries a gun just in case."

A gun is a gun. Its implication is in its design. While a gun can provide a sense of safety and security, it does so through threat, or act of violence. It can only be used for good if the person holding it is actually willing to pull the trigger.

When we use the word *control* to define the sovereignty of God, we put a gun in His hand.

If we insist that God's sovereignty has something to do with control, then whenever He interacts in our lives, He is being sovereignly controlling. Actually, everything we experience, be it positive or negative, must be attributed in some way to His controlling nature.

Much of the Church believes *God is in absolute control* and also that *God is always good.* These two opposing thoughts have positioned many believers in a fractured, compromised state where their faith can become undermined by circumstances and disappointments.

A good God in control forces us to justify the Tsunami as God's will, and then we are left with how to navigate the aftermath.

The sinner that died? Well, that was a just God acting from sovereign control.

The six-month-old who drowned? Well, that was a horrible tragedy… or was it more? Was it somehow God's will? You just never know…

And trust is eroded…

Lunch with Mark

The restaurant was quiet, we were well passed the noon rush. And we were well passed caught up; wives and kids, travels and mutual friends, daily hurdles and breakthroughs all discussed, our salads long gone, our pasta a happy memory.

Satisfied, we sipped our second coffee while we reveled in our friendship and the goodness of God. Back and forth we shared God stories, stirring and encouraging each other. Eventually our conversation landed on this book and the tension I was feeling in writing it.

I had experienced some push back from unnerved pastors, uncomfortable friends, and downright angry strangers; all beautiful sons and daughters.

"Jason, years ago when you first told me about this book, I was both excited and uncomfortable!" Mark said.

I smiled, "I remember. I was too."

Mark laughed. "I know you are feeling tension, and rightfully so. What you are writing addresses a belief firmly held by many; a belief that has become an institution unto itself, unalterable and beyond review."

Mark paused and then his demeanor shifted. He became sober and earnest, "But let me tell you why you must finish this book."

Mark Appleyard is a man of wisdom and encouragement. He is a good friend. He pastors a church near where I live and leads an international ministry to business leaders around the globe.[5] He is a man of great insight.

He had my attention.

"Jason, this book? It's about trust." When Mark said that, my heart leapt.

He continued, "I believe what you are writing has the potential to empower life transforming trust and lead people into great intimacy."

Marks encouragement was huge. You see, this book was not written to convince you that God is not in control, this book was written to reveal the perfection of God's love for you. My hope is that those who read this might access greater trust and grow in intimacy.

Created for Intimacy

"How do I experience God's love?"

Because I write and speak on the always good love of our heavenly Father, that is a question I am asked often. It's a question I believe many sons and daughters have wrestled with, particularly in the Western Church where many have had to puzzle out God's role in the devastation

[5]*For more information on the ministry of Mark Appleyard go to www.anothen.co*

of the most recent Tsunami…

Much of the church has had to navigate the insecurity inherent in a theology of control. I believe this has birthed a great crisis regarding intimacy with God; we don't know how to experience His pleasure. We have little access to His good love.

Many of us know the names of God, we know His attributes, we are intellectually certain He loves us, and yet we are not confident in His affection. While we all desire closeness with God, for many, closeness with God is far from a daily, moment by moment, experience.

For many, the Christian faith is based more on an acknowledgement of God's love than an actual encounter. But love goes beyond intellect; love is an emotive experience with a Person.

Have you ever noticed that at least two thirds of the Kingdom can be felt? *"For the Kingdom of God is not a matter of what we eat or drink, but of living a life of goodness and peace and joy in the Holy Spirit."*[6]

This scripture in Romans reveals that the Kingdom can be emotionally experienced. *Joy* and *peace* are not just theological positions in God; they are also actual felt responses to experiencing His presence.

We are designed to experience God's presence, His closeness, His affection. He created us for relationship; not a theoretical relationship, but an experiential knowing. We were born to know and be known, to commune with God, to have an honest, true, whole, authentic, affectionate relationship with our Savior and Friend.

It's called intimacy.

And I would like to propose that much of the church is unable to access this intimacy for one reason. We have a theology of control.

Intimacy and Control

Control can be a good concept when applied to things or situations.

---

[6]*Romans 14:17 NLT*

Jason was in control of the car. That's good.

But control is a broken idea when applied to relationship, it undermines intimacy.

Jason was in control of his wife, his kids, his friends, his parents, his neighbors, his subjects... That's not good.

Intimacy can't be experienced in a relationship where one person is controlling the other. Intimacy is only experienced where there is trust. And trust isn't possible if one of the people in a relationship carries a gun...just in case.

You can't have intimacy with someone you can't trust. And control undermines trust. It is the antithesis of intimacy.

A God-in-control positions humanity in insecurity. It undermines trust in the One who we are most designed to know and trust. Why? Because a God in control is a controlling God.

A theology of sovereign control erodes our ability to trust, making intimacy with God something we are promised but never fully experience.

But Jesus powerfully modeled the way into intimacy by surrendering His very life. Jesus rejected the gun; the very idea of control.

If we aren't convinced that God is love and His love is sovereign, perfectly good; if we think God is in control of particular areas of our lives, then we are forced to navigate those areas of our lives outside of intimacy. And it effects everything!

The Subtle Erosions of Control

The theology of sovereign control doesn't just undermine our faith in God's good love when facing tsunami-size problems; it subtlety erodes access to trust in our everyday life.

If He is in control, then when we stub our toe, the car needs new brakes and we don't have the cash, the neighbor doesn't like us, someone else gets the closer parking space, the dog escapes from the backyard and it's getting dark and he's not that bright; even in the subtle context of daily life, we are forced to wrestle over something that is (and should be in our minds) an absolute – the goodness of God. Ultimately our trust is compromised and intimacy is lost.

We are designed to live, move and have our being in the confidence that He is always good – that His love is sovereign. And yet our misguided definition of His sovereignty undermines our ability to trust in His goodness. Our faith is subverted by our misunderstanding.

But, if we are willing to step away from the flawed narrative of control and lean into a greater revelation of His love, it opens up for us an opportunity to trust His goodness in ways we have never been able to trust before.

And in this trust, we will begin to know His affection in ways we have never fully known, but always longed for. And when we begin to discover His affection truly and fully, we will experience intimacy with God.

Jesus came to make us sure. Jesus revealed sovereign love and He came to give us access to intimacy.

The whole world needs to know this!

A Measureless Invitation

Control is a word that defines a great deal in the finite understanding of earth. It is a word that can be used for good. It can make us feel safe and secure.

Again, "*Jason is in control of the car,*" is a good thing.

Of course, truly, Jason is not in control of the car unless he is first in control of himself. But more on that later.

I understand that the concept of control makes sense on earth. But I am not writing about the math of earth. This book is about the measureless revelation of heaven. While control is the vocabulary of our finite physical story, this book is an invitation to the whole story.

You see, control is a finite word in a finite language among thousands of finite languages. But Love is a Person, an infinite revelation.

Control will end, but Love has no beginning and no end, Love has always been and will always be.

Control is a perspective to articulate measurement. It can't be applied to a measureless revelation. God is love. Love is immeasurable.

Jesus was the unravelling revelation into another way of thinking and perceiving. He was a re-introduction to our native tongue. He made it possible for us to be re-born so we might re-discover. When Jesus walked the earth, He redeemed our narrative so we could once again live in the finite from the infinite. At this exact moment, we are actually seated in Christ at the right hand of the Father.[7]

So please understand, when I write, "God is not in control," I am addressing a finite perspective with an infinite revelation. And the good news is, in Christ, it's possible for us to discover this revelation. You see, the infinite lives inside of us!

While God placed us in a world defined by measurements, He breathed His Spirit, the measureless revelation of love, into us. So, while we live in the insecurities of this earth, we have been invited to live from the confidence of heaven.

I understand that the idea of a God in control can make us feel secure when we live in a fallen world defined by measurements. But it's just not true. God is not in control, it's infinitely better than that, God is love. And He is continually inviting us into this measureless revelation so we might live like Jesus, secure, on earth as it is in heaven.

At the end of the day, I am not trying to convince you that the concept of control doesn't hold some merit here on earth. But this book isn't about math, it's about love, it's about trust and intimacy.

---

[7]*See Ephesians 2:6 & Mark 16:19*

Stubbornly Convinced

Long before I wrote the last sentence of this book, like I have done before, I sent the manuscript to family and friends for feedback. This time I wasn't caught by surprise with some of the uncomfortable, unsettled responses.

One friend, after reading a few pages, sent a kind-hearted email response suggesting that maybe I was stubbornly splitting hairs; that the terms *sovereign love* and *sovereign control* both worked when describing Gods nature.

"You say po-tay-toe I say po-tot-o, let's call the whole thing off."

You know, semantics.

It's true, I can be stubborn.

The problem is, it's not semantics, it's a matter of His goodness and our access to intimacy.

I am stubbornly convinced there is a vast difference between a theology of *love* and a theology of *control.*

I am stubbornly convinced that knowing God as sovereign love leads to greater trust and intimacy. And I'm equally stubbornly convinced that believing God is sovereignly in control undermines our trust and stifles our access to intimacy.

Please know, it's my heart that the ultimate take away from this book is not, *God is not in control*; it's, *God is love, His love is always good and we exist to grow sure.*

This book is not a thesis on control, it's an invitation to a potential new thought about the wonder and power and perfection of God's love. It's an invitation to re-discover our native tongue. It's an invitation to greater trust and intimacy.

Of this I am becoming convinced, God is sovereign but He doesn't carry a gun, He is not in control. And I would like to suggest that any universe held together by a God with a gun needs some stubborn unraveling.

And so, I'll continue to pull the string.

Are you feeling brave enough to continue journeying with me?

chapter five
THE WHOLE STORY

Niagara

Had she the ability at the time to articulate with words, she would have said I was acting like a controlling sovereign. Instead, she just screamed, arched her back, kicked her legs and started crying. She acted just like a two-year-old.

My two-year-old girl, Madi, in her 'infinite' wisdom, had determined we weren't close enough to the river. She was furious.

So was the river. It rushed past with a singleness of purpose - to plunge the depth and reunite with the rock-strewn riverbed almost two hundred feet below.

Niagara Falls is awe-inspiring. And Madi was not content to peek over the railing mere feet from the edge. She wanted to taste and touch.

As I literally wrestled her fingers from the railing, she made it piercingly clear to everyone, including the senior citizen bus tour nearby, that I was unkind, withholding, a controlling brute of a man.

Control. That's the word I imagine she would have used. And to be fair, from her perspective, it was true. I controlled her. To Madi, it felt like I didn't care, like I was denying her some wonderful experience...

Of course, it was just the opposite.

Everything about our Niagara outing had been done with Madi in mind. Her mom and I had dressed her so she would be warm, dry and protected. We had taken her to the edge so she could see this most awe-inspiring wonder. We held her secure while she looked on in amazement.

The whole day had been designed to give her a new experience, to enlarge her world, to expand her wonder and her thinking.

The fact is, Madi's mom and I are the two people on the planet who most love and adore her. We have planned and cared for our beautiful girl since before she was born. We dream of a future where she has access to everything she needs in order to succeed in life, to experience grace and joy and peace and love. That's our desire for all our kids.

In parenting, our motivation has never been to control our kids, just the opposite; we want to empower our kids to control themselves. But self-control is a learning process. And some days, successful parenting is simply determined by the fact that we all survived.

That's why on that brisk Niagara Falls day I forcefully carried Madi away from the real possibility of a cold, swift, terrifyingly painful death.

Not counting the busload of senior citizens, there are two perspectives in this story, two narratives - my daughter's and mine.

My daughter's perspective – I controlled her.

My perspective – I loved her.

Was my daughter's perspective wrong? No, it was just immature. Was there truth in her narrative? If she were solely describing her understanding and how she felt at that moment, then yes, but it was certainly not the truth that would set her free.

Was control a part of her story? At the time, she would have described it that way, but only because, at two years of age, she was too immature to understand the whole story. And let's be honest, the whole story is the true story.

Of all the ways to describe my actions that day at the Falls, *"control"* would be the most immature way. And it's the same for us when, in our own life experiences, we attribute control to God's nature.

Immaturity isn't necessarily wrong; it's simply life in its formative days. But the thoughts we form about God in those days determine everything that follows. If, in our formative days, we commit to the idea that a controlling sovereign is the whole story, then we will actually stifle our maturing process and stunt our spiritual growth. We will actually remain immature. Ultimately, it will greatly affect the nature of our relationship to God our Father.

If Madi, or any of our kids, were to grow up believing control was their parents motivation and intention, it would ultimately undermine our relationship with them. Eventually they would begin to chafe under their flawed perception and seek to set themselves free.

A theology of control is an immature perspective that will birth distrust and lead us into rebellion or striving; into *secular thought* or *religious thought* – to what seems right to a man.[1] Ultimately, it will undermine an intimate connection with our heavenly Father and lead to living with the mindset of a slave.

The Parable of the Prodigal

This story may be familiar to you.

There was a father with two immature sons. The young son perceived his father as controlling; life was too restrictive under his father's roof. He had this foolish desire to go swimming in the Niagara River, or something like that.

---

[1]*Proverbs 14:12,* NIV

So the young fella became a prodigal son, "*wasteful and reckless*."[2] He left the perceived controls of his fathers' house, taking with him his share of the inheritance and spending it in every immature, self-centered way conceivable. Then this prodigal son experienced the consequences of his decisions – the violence of Niagara Falls. He fell upon financial hard times and he lost everything.

Destitute and desperate, he took a job feeding pigs. When he realized that the pigs ate better than he did, he fondly remembered home, how the servants in his father's house ate well, were warm and dry, and all around better off. He realized his father was a good master, generous and kind to his servants.

This *revelation* was profound, especially considering his circumstances.

In his great despair, he caught a glimpse of the whole story, a truth that could set him free. What was that truth? His father was a good master. This softened and humbled the young prodigals heart.

He repented.

That's how repentance works; it's a revelation of the kindness of God that leads us to repent, to change the way we think. It's found in Romans 2:4

The young son decided to return home and beg forgiveness in hopes he might be given a job as a servant in his father's house. Jesus tells this story in Luke 15 - minus the Niagara references. It's known as *The Parable of the Prodigal Son*. If you've read it, then you remember what happens next.

As the son neared home, while still on the road, the good father ran out to meet him. There was no shaming, no anger, no mention of his sons past, and no demand for reparation. The good father greeted his son with overwhelming joy, mercy and grace; his forgiveness so generously complete.

---

[2]*Dictionary.com*

The son didn't even have the chance to request a position as a servant. Instead, he experienced perfect love and suddenly he had his father's perspective, the whole story. He saw what had always been; his father was good and kind.

This was a profound moment of clarity where the son realized that control was not in the nature of his father, it had simply been the flawed perspective of an immature son.

No longer a prodigal, the son transitioned in how he related to his father; he moved from acting like a slave to acting like a son, from a control narrative, to love. He changed the way he thought; his mind was renewed and he was transformed.

That's how transformation works; we are transformed by the renewing of our minds, by changing the way we think. It's found in Romans 12:2.

What I love about this story is that the prodigal son returned home with a surrendered heart in hopes of serving a good master only to discoverer a greater revelation, the whole story, a truer narrative... the loving arms of his good father.

And I would like to propose we have all been invited to take the same transformational journey. To navigate from our perspective to His, from our story to the whole story...

To See How He See's

When my daughter Eva was an infant, and even into her toddler days, she had an all-consuming attachment to her momma. Karen rarely went anywhere without her, that includes laundry rooms, bedrooms and even bathrooms.

When Karen needed to leave the house without Eva, we had to be very strategic regarding her exit. Otherwise we could have a potential near nuclear crisis on our hands.

And then there were the occasions when Karen, without thinking, would decide to get the mail! She would simply walk out the front door – without Eva! I know!

The mailbox was only 25 feet from the house and it would take no more than a minute before she returned. But if Eva happened to see Karen leave...

The sounds she made would break your heart.

And I would come running. I would scoop her up, hold her close and whisper, "It's ok honey, Daddy's got you. Momma is coming right back."

Even though I like to tell my kids that I just may be the world's greatest father, none of them would describe me as long suffering. But even at my most impatient, I was never annoyed or angered by Eva's tears. I never belittled her inability to comprehend the situation.

As her loving dad, I recognized my little girl didn't understand that her momma was just outside the door. I was able to see from her perspective and value it. I positioned myself in her pain, I acted with compassion, kindness, maturity and love.

"Daddy loves you, it's gonna be alright,"

While I soothed her heart, I carried her to the front door window. Why? So I could give her access to my perspective. I would point out Karen. "Look, there she is! Can you see mommy?"

You see, while I fully immersed myself in her story, I also invited her into the whole story.

My point? God is infinitely better at Fathering than I am.

In our immaturity, we may perceive God and our life through the lens of our heartbreak, disappointment, vanity, self-reliance... the list is long. But all along the way He is the loving Father running to us, scooping us up, positioning Himself in our pain, immersing Himself in our story.

He is compassionate, kind, mature and loving. And all along the way

He is inviting us to transition from our perspective to His, from our story to the whole story.

Master and Father

I believe Jesus told this parable of the prodigal son for one reason; He was transitioning us from one narrative to another; moving us from a theology of control to theology of love. He was revealing His perspective on what it means to be a servant by introducing the revelation of family.

Jesus, *"Who, being in very nature God, did not consider equality with God something to be used to his own advantage; rather, he made himself nothing by taking the very nature of a servant, being made in human likeness." Philippians 2:6-7*

And Jesus, living as the perfect expression of a servant, called His Master, *Dad.* Please get this; for thirty-three years Jesus perfectly revealed what it looks like to be a servant by living confident as a beloved Son. Jesus showed us the whole story. The life of a believer wasn't just about being a servant to a good Master, it was infinitely better than that. The life of a believer was about being a son or daughter to a good Father, it was about Family.

Jesus revealed that surrendering to God, as a *good Master,* is the foundational invitation into a revelation of our *good heavenly Father.* It's the narrow road that leads to the vast landscape of His Kingdom come, the narrow gate that empowers a measureless revelation of His love, the doorway through which we transition from one narrative into another.[3]

Jesus was always revealing that *God, as a good Master* is just the beginning of our story, there is so much more!

What I am trying to communicate is simply this, the point of the prodigal son story wasn't just to note a young man's enlightenment regarding the difference between good masters and bad masters.

No, the point of this story is that the prodigal son, the kid who had grown up in a world defined by masters and slaves, the kid who

---

[3]*See Matthew 7:14,* NIV

immaturely perceived his father as controlling, the kid who had lived under the good master's roof with a slave mindset, the kid who had willfully left the good master's house, would discover a greater revelation, a truer narrative... his father's good love and the revelation of family.

This parable was an invitation to transition. It was an introduction to the whole story. One in which we could call our Master, Abba, Daddy, Father.

The truth that God is a good Master is the foundational starting place, but it is never meant to be the destination. Knowing God as a good Master should always lead to the greater revelation of God as our good and loving Father. If it doesn't, we have missed the point, the whole story, the truth that sets us free.

The fact is, a revelation of God as a good Master can draw a prodigal servant home, but only the greater revelation of God as a good Father can secure and empower a son or daughter to live like Christ.

Jesus revealed the whole story and it was infinitely better than being a slave to a good master. It was about relationship; it was about family. It always is. And this family perspective brings such clarity and beauty to words like slave or servant...

Now you probably already know this, but the prodigal son story didn't end with the return of the younger son. This father had two sons.

The Older Son

The older son was furious when he came in from working the fields to discover his father had thrown a celebration party for his newly-returned foolish younger brother. He couldn't fathom how his father would honor a selfish, disobedient, and undisciplined slave. We know this by what he said to his father when he was urged to join in the celebration.

"'Look! All these years I've been slaving for you and never disobeyed your orders. Yet you never gave me even a young goat so I could celebrate with my friends.'"[4]

---

[4]*See Luke 15:25-31,* NIV

The older son lived immaturely enslaved to the same perceived controls his younger brother had left home to escape. While the younger went off to engage in his immature understanding of freedom, the older brother chose to stay and slave under his master's roof. Along the way resentment built; his heart became hard and he became blind to his father's perspective.

This slave mindset ended up defining all his relationships and the older brother became religious. *Good behavior* became his true master. *Striving* became his gospel. The fact is, even though he stayed home, he was nearly as lost as his prodigal brother had been.

Upon seeing his younger brother celebrated, the older son also experienced the violence of Niagara Falls. His paradigm was shaken to its core.

Then, his father revealed the whole story, his perspective, *"My son,' the father said, 'you are always with me, and everything I have is yours."*[5]

Essentially, the father was saying, "You want a goat? All my goats are your goats, and my cows, and my pigs, my fields, my houses, my influence, my favor, my authority, everything that's mine is yours..."

"*Everything I have, all that I am, is yours*" was the same greater revelation that had so transformed the younger brother just hours earlier. This was the whole story that would empower and set free.

Sadly, the religious, self-righteous mindset is a much harder *control* to be free of. Jesus explained it kind of like this, "*...it's easier for a camel to go through the eye of a needle...*"[6] than for a religiously self-righteous man to repent; to change the way he thinks.

The older brother would not humble himself; he would not repent.

I would like to propose that if we insist on viewing God as a controlling master, we will either find ourselves like the prodigal, enslaved to *secular thought* outside the house, or we will find ourselves like the older brother, enslaved to *religious thought* inside the house.

---

[5]*Luke 15:31,* NIV
[6]*See Mark 10:25,* NIV

Either way, we become bound to thinking and acting like a slave.

Christ's Slave?

Let's be very clear, slavery is an abomination; it's a mindset against the revelation of Jesus. Slavery is a fallen-world system birthed from a theology of control. It didn't exist before the fall and doesn't exist in heaven. It is a reality in absolute opposition to sovereign love.

When Adam chose *the knowledge of good and evil* he introduced slavery into every human experience. But Jesus redeemed the narrative, He set us free!

So, what do we do with what Paul writes about himself in Romans 1:1, *"Paul, a servant of Christ Jesus, called to be an apostle and set apart for the gospel of God."*

What about 1st Corinthians 7:22, when Paul writes, "*...the one who was free when called is Christ's slave.*"

These verses and more can be confusing if we don't realize that the good Master Paul is serving is also the good Father Jesus revealed in the Parable of the Prodigal Son. They are one and the same!

The fact is, when Paul wrote as a slave, he never left his position as a beloved son to his good Father. Paul wrote as a son, describing, with great maturity, the freedom and transformation he had experienced in absolute surrender to sovereign Love.

Paul was not saying, *"God is in control of me,"* he was saying, *"I freely and joyfully lay my life down at His feet."*

Paul was not saying, *"My Master makes me do things I don't want to do."* He was saying, *"I only want to do the things that are on my Father's heart."*

Paul was not saying, *"I have no choice, I must obey my Master's demands."* He was saying, *"I only desire to do the will of my Father."*

Jesus displayed perfectly what a son surrendered to a good Father looked like when He said, "*Very truly I tell you, the Son can do nothing by himself; he can do only what he sees his Father doing, because whatever the Father does the Son also does.*"[7]

Jesus wasn't saying "*My Master is in control of me.*" He was saying, "*I freely and whole heartedly surrender my will to my Fathers.*"

He wasn't saying, "*I have to do what my Master tells me.*" He was saying, "*It is my joy and passion to only do what is on my Fathers heart.*"

Jesus was never once forced by His Father to surrender His will to His Father's. Even when He laid His life down, He did it voluntarily. "*No one takes it from me, but I lay it down of my own accord...*"[8]

There are two types of surrender, forced or voluntary. God has never once forced us to surrender. That's not how love works. Sovereign love doesn't demand control, it empowers freedom, reveals kindness, restores trust and invites surrender.

And surrendering to sovereign love is an act of maturity. It leads to a powerful paradigm shift. It transitions us from our perspective to our Father's perspective – the truth that sets us free.

Maturity is the ability to see from another's perspective. And when we see from our Father's perspective, suddenly we aren't laboring, we're co-laboring; we aren't slaving, we're walking in obedient surrender, whole heartedly as beloved sons and daughters.

Obedience

There are two ways by which to know and obey God. Control or love.

If we have a theology of control, then our obedience will be about giving God control. This was the mindset of both brothers. The younger became reckless and rebellious. The order became distrustful and self-righteous.

---

[7]*John 5:19*, NIV
[8]*John 10:18*, NIV

Either way, the control perspective led to striving and undermined an intimate connection with their father. It stunted their maturity and led to thinking and acting like slaves instead of sons.

If we have a theology of love, then our obedience will lead to transformation. When God asks us to obey, it is an invitation to trust and discover His perspective, the whole story. Obedience is an invitation to mature and live sure as a son or daughter.

You see, obedience is never about giving God control. Obedience is a decision made in freedom to voluntarily surrender our will to His. Obedience is the evidence of self-control.

Obedience, in love, leads to sons and daughters growing sure. It is an act of maturity that empowers us to see how our Father sees, love the way He loves, and become like Him.

Family Is the Kingdom

What if the whole story is infinitely better than a master in control because it's about a good Father who loves. What if the whole story is about family, about sons and daughters growing sure in their Fathers affection, living powerfully free as mature expressions of His Kingdom come?

Family is the Kingdom Jesus talked about, the Kingdom He lived from, the Kingdom He revealed, the Kingdom He taught us to pray for and invited us to discover here *on earth as it is in heaven.* And this Kingdom expression of family is experienced through voluntary surrender to the good Master and the discovery of our Father's sovereign love.

From the moment we said yes to Christ, we were invited to mature, to grow sure in love, in trust, in the discovery of our Father's good love. Jesus made it plain; the revelation of a good Master should always lead to the revelation of a good Father.

The good Master is our good Father! Living as a servant in the context of family transitions us from one narrative to another. It shifts us from control to freedom.

We were designed for freedom. But if we are unwilling to transition from control to love, we will wrestle with slaving, either through rebellion or striving. If we rebel, then, we will eventually find ourselves feeding pigs, lost and nearly dead in our desperation. If we strive, then we will eventually find ourselves resentful, self-righteous, powerless and nearly dead in our affection.

I would like to suggest that control is an immature and powerless way to know God, it is a flawed perspective regarding His sovereignty. I would like to suggest that control is not in God's nature, it's in man's perception.

Control is not the whole story and therefore not the true story. It won't set us free, just the opposite. If we maintain a theology of control we will continually be positioned practically and experientially as servants and only theoretically as sons and daughters.

When we serve a controlling God, we set up barriers between us and the full family relationship Jesus purchased and revealed; barriers to fully experiencing the closeness of our Father's affection, the wonder of knowing Jesus as a brother, the absolute joy in friendship with Holy Spirit.

Knowing God as a good Father is the whole story. It empowers us to see the world the way He sees, we begin to recognize His goodness in everything; we are transformed and along the way we mature.

Knowing God as the good Father is filled with exponential freedom, exponential life, exponential righteousness, peace, joy, trust, authority, and power. When we know the good Father, we live in the inheritance of sons and daughters, in the measureless revelation of sovereign love.

chapter six
THE ZEBRA

The Zebra

I was recently at a service where the speaker told a fable. It went something like this.

There were four fellas; they each wore different-colored glasses, red, blue, yellow and green. They stood at the edge of a field; in the distance was a zebra. They were each asked to describe the color of the zebra.

As one would expect, the guy with the red glasses saw a red and black zebra; the guy with the blue glasses, blue and black. So, it went, yellow, and green, each seeing the zebra through their lenses, in their respective colors.

The speaker then presented a question to us, "Who is correct regarding the true color of the zebra?" He paused long enough for me to have the thought, "Zebras are white and black."

But that wasn't the question.

"Who knows the true color of the zebra?" the speaker asked again and then he answered.

"The zebra."

What the Hell?

I remember the first time I read about how David won a battle against the Moabites and after the battle *"he made them (the Moabites) lie down on the ground and measured them off with a length of cord. Every two lengths of them were put to death, and the third length was allowed to live. So the Moabites became subject to David and brought him tribute." Samuel 81:2*

When I finished reading this I literally said out loud, "What the hell?"

Seriously, what the hell?

This story is just a paragraph in the many chapters of David's incredible life. It's a seemingly insignificant footnote, unless you were a Moabite, then it's a story of horrifying slaughter. And oddly, the author apparently didn't feel the need to enlighten us as to how David came to this seemingly random approach to flirting with genocide.

This cold-blooded brutality, this almost casual annihilation of entire people groups; it's everywhere in the Old Testament. And what's most disconcerting, as often as not, God seems to be credited as the primary instigator.

Moses writes about it a good deal. In fact, he's the guy who "penned" the famous story of Noah. You know, the story where God seems keen on killing everyone.

"The LORD regretted that he had made human beings on the earth, and his heart was deeply troubled. So the LORD said, "I will wipe from the face of the earth the human race I have created—and with them the animals, the birds and the creatures that move along the ground—for I regret that I have made them." Genesis 5:6-8

What the hell?

The Old Testament is littered with stories like this one. Stories where humanity is depraved, and God is angry, and destruction is imminent, and then often realized.

Then, to the wonder and eternal gratitude of all of us, Jesus is introduced into the narrative. And with His arrival, God's thoughts about us suddenly seem to change.

In the Old Testament, *"If a man is found sleeping with another man's wife, both the man who slept with her and the woman must die."*[1] And yet, in the New Testament, when a woman, caught in adultery, is thrown at Jesus feet, He says, "*neither do I condemn you*"[2] and He forgives her.

In the Old Testament, God *"hates all who do wrong."*[3] In the New Testament, He fellowshipped with sinners. He dined with them, laughed and cried with them, He delivered, healed and saved them. I can't think of any stories where He killed them. I don't think it happened even once.

So yeah, I'm not the first person to notice that the God of the Old Testament seems to be very different from the God Jesus revealed in the New. The disparity is enough to make one think God was either seriously manic for a long time, or He is fickle, changing like the wind. But then we read Malachi 3:6, *"I the Lord do not change..."*

And so, we're left with the question, *"if God didn't change, what did?"*

Perspective

2000 years ago, Jesus walked the earth and for the first time we saw God as He truly was. And God was way different than we thought. He wasn't a controlling deity disappointed by our stumbling. He didn't seem outraged by our brokenness, by our sin. He wasn't in a bad mood. He wasn't angry, at least not in the vengeful way the writers of the Old Testament seemed to portray Him. He didn't smite anyone, didn't even seem to want to.

Yes, He strongly addressed lack of faith. Yes, He challenged all

---

[1]*See Deuteronomy 22:22,* NIV
[2]*See John 8:11,* NIV
[3]*See Psalms 5:5,* NIV

humanity to wholehearted surrender. And yes, one time He even used a whip to drive the money lenders out of the temple grounds. But there were no deaths, not even a report of injury - just hurt pride.

Don't get me wrong, Jesus did get angry.

But when Jesus *was* angry, it was with the religious leaders; the self-righteous who sought control like the drug it is; the self-serving who used the theology of control to oppress others; those who shamed and condemned in His name; those who wielded control like a sword. Yet, while He used some strong language when confronting or describing them, "*brood of vipers,*" "*blind guides,*" "*fools*" and "*hypocrites,*"[4] even then, He never once followed it up with a killing spree.

Jesus never once had people put down in the dirt, divided into thirds, and then had two out of every three slaughtered where they lay.

The stories of God and mass killings seem to be missing from the four Gospels; the four books in which God is most clearly revealed. Oddly, the clearest revelation of God, the perfect picture of sovereignty, seems to be missing the angry, murderous, destructive bent.

And no one seemed to understand.

Jesus lived absolutely counter to religious culture, He turned the world upside down. The last were first, the poor were rich, the meek inherited the earth, the weak became strong, sinners were loved, prostitutes forgiven, and willful prodigals greeted with a kiss – none of it made sense.

Jesus, revealing God for who He truly is, walked as the perfect expression of sovereign love. And everyone was baffled by it.

I would like to propose that the reason no one could truly comprehend was because all humanity wore colored glasses.

They saw everything, including Jesus, through the lens of sovereign control. It's not surprising - control had been the prevailing perspective since the fall.

---

[4]*See Matthew 12:23, Matthew 15:14, Matthew 5:22, & Matthew 23:13*

Even Jesus disciples, those who had never once witnessed Jesus do anything that smacks remotely of genocide, were wearing shades.

"When the days were approaching for His ascension, He (Jesus) was determined to go to Jerusalem; and He sent messengers on ahead of Him, and they went and entered a village of the Samaritans to make arrangements for Him. But they did not receive Him, because He was traveling toward Jerusalem.

When His disciples James and John saw this, they said, "Lord, do You want us to command fire to come down from heaven and consume them?" But He turned and said..."

"What the hell?"

I'm not being trite, nor trying to offend. I believe hell is a pretty accurate word to expose the spirit behind the disciple's thinking...

"...But He turned and said, 'You do not know what kind of spirit you are of; for the Son of Man did not come to destroy men's lives, but to save them.'"[5]

If you want the clearest understanding regarding God's heart for humanity, this scripture is a good place to start. In fact, it's the point of this entire chapter.

Long ago, I made Jesus, sovereign love, my hermeneutic, my *"methodology of interpretation,"*[6] the lens through which my entire theology is defined. But the disciples hadn't gotten there yet...

Jesus essentially says to his *hell fire* disciples, "Fellas, your theology is really messed up, your lenses are colored, your perspective of who I am is horribly flawed! For nearly three years you have witnessed me save, heal, deliver, forgive, redeem, restore and empower. Never once did I use fire and brimstone. Guys, the spirit behind your desire to see destruction reigned down is in direct opposition to everything I have been revealing. Seriously, the control lens through which you perceive me is from the pit of hell."

---

[5]*Luke 9:51-56*, NIV

[6]*Wikipedia description of the word "hermeneutic."*

Then Jesus continued to perfectly reveal sovereign Love in His dealings with humanity by journeying on to the cross and to resurrection life.

And He completely changed the way we could know what God looked and acted like. No longer did we have to interpret Him through a theology of control, now we could know Him through the revelation of love.

Jesus is the lens.

He revealed a truer narrative and with it humanity gained access to the whole story. We can truly see God, from Old Testament through the New. We can truly discover sovereignty, we can truly trust Him, we can truly be free.

My point, it wasn't God that changed from Old Testament to New, it was our perspective. Or more accurately, our perspective can change, if we choose to make Jesus, sovereign love, the lens, *"the author and perfecter of our faith."*[7]

You see, until Jesus, we had bits and pieces of the story, God inspired fragments. The Old Testament writers revealed God like the zebra in a field. Some said, "He is red with black stripes." Some said, "He is blue; still others said yellow and green." Then God walked among us in the flesh and revealed Himself perfectly.

"Who knows the true color of the zebra?"

Jesus.

I believe Jesus is the whole story. He is the lens through which I can truly know God. And He is the lens through which I read the Old Testament.

For me, interpreting the Old Testament outside the revelation of Jesus is to completely miss the point. It's foolish. It would be like watching the first pre-season game of the Buffalo Bills and then buying tickets to watch them play in the Super Bowl.

---

[7]*See Hebrews 12:2*

I am convinced that Jesus is the lens by which we interpret the Old Testament and the New. And I have discovered that when I read through the lens of sovereign love, suddenly a story about a flood that wipes out nearly all of humanity doesn't make me desperate or insecure.

It has always been God's heart that none would perish.[8]

Always...

God Inspired and Moses Interpreted

Moses is the fella credited to have most likely written what would have already been the age-old story of Noah; a story that had been orally passed down from generation to generation.

Moses was one hundred percent inspired of God when he wrote the first five books regarding the relationship between God and man. And what Moses wrote was an absolutely true story. But I would like to suggest it was not the whole story. Moses didn't have the whole story yet; he wasn't looking at God and man through the perfect lens of sovereign love; the lens revealed in Jesus life, death and resurrection.

Therefore, while Moses' perspective was fully inspired of God, was powerful and good, I would like to propose it was not definitive; it was not complete.

When it comes to Noah's story, God inspired and Moses interpreted the inspiration. And I would like to suggest that Moses had a theology, a context, a paradigm, a narrative, a lens – sovereign control.

In the sovereign control narrative of Moses' day, it was determined that if you touched a leper you were made unclean.[9] In the sovereign love narrative, Jesus revealed the whole story. When He touched a leper, the leper was made clean.[10]

In the control perspective of Moses' day, punishment was the language of God. Moses captured this well when He wrote on God's behalf "*...I will wipe from the face of the earth the human race I have created.*"

---

[8]*See 2 Peter 3:9*
[9]*Leviticus 13:45,* NIV
[10]*Matthew 8:3,* NIV

However, Jesus revealed the whole story, a truer perspective, the language of forgiveness and redemption, when He said, *"...for the Son of Man did not come to destroy men's lives, but to save them."*

Here's what I am trying to convey, Moses saw the zebra in a field, he described it truly through the lens he had, sovereign control. He described it truly but not definitively, not completely. He captured the problem but not the solution, he wrote down the story, but it wasn't the whole story.

Then Jesus came and gave us perfect 20/20 vision regarding what God was like, sovereign love. And Jesus also made it clear how to read the whole Bible.

"You study the scriptures because you think in them is eternal life but they testify of me."[11]

Jesus wasn't talking about the New Testament; it hadn't been written yet. He was specifically addressing how to interpret the Old Testament. His point was that scripture wasn't the answer, it pointed to the answer. And He was also making it clear, He was that answer.

Jesus is *"the word made flesh"*[12] He is the interpretation.

Scripture tells a story, scripture paints a picture of a Zebra in a field, it describes what the zebra is like.

But who truly knows the color of a zebra?

The Zebra.

I believe every word of the Bible is inspired of God. God inspired and men wrote it down. But the Bible is not a part of the Trinity. The Bible isn't God, it reveals Him. And we all have a God lens. And that lens determines everything.

What If...

What if we read the story of Noah through the interpretation of

---

[11]*John 5:39,* NAS
[12]*See John 1:4*

Jesus? What if we applied God's heart not "*to destroy men's lives, but to save them*" to that epic tale? Is it possible we might see it differently?

What if the depravity of sin was so devastating in Noah's day that humanity and innocence was being consumed? What if "*every inclination of the thoughts of the human heart was only evil all the time.*"[13] What if the earth "*was corrupt*" and "*full of violence?*"[14] What if, like Paul notes in Romans 8, "*all creation*" groaned under the weight of sin and death?[15]

What if this groaning of a broken and fallen earth erupted in the form of an all-consuming flood? What if God, in His saving mercy, gave humanity a 120-year warning by sending a message to the one man on the planet who was living in such a way that he could hear it.

What if, for the next 120 years, Noah built an ark by God's instruction, grace and provision? What if the feat was an act of faith like none seen before on the planet? What if the construction was supernaturally ahead of its time in design and engineering?

What if the people lived in the shadow of this magnificent testimony of God's desire to save them for 120 years and yet not one person repented, not one heart softened?

And what if the people would have humbled themselves and prayed, and sought His face, and turned from their wicked ways? Is it possible He would have forgiven their sin and healed their land?[16]

What if God, who was perfectly revealed in Jesus, does not change? What if it has never been His heart "*to destroy men's lives,*" and it has always been His heart "*to save them,*" even during the time of Noah's flood?

Floods

Noah's story is incredible. He lived faithfully obedient in the context of sovereign control. But I want to highlight the difference between Noah's navigation of a flood and how we have been set free to navigate a flood today.

---

[13]*See Genesis 6:5,* NIV

[14]*See Genesis 6:11,* NIV

[15]*See Romans 8:20-22,* NIV

[16]*See 2 Chronicles 7:14*

I want to suggest that the clarity of our perception determines everything.

Noah's lens on God was not definitive, He did not have the revelation of Christ, a redeemed perspective, the whole story. For Noah, God was sovereignly in control and in a control narrative, the flood was perceived as God's wrathful punishment of a horrendously sinful people. It was something to be survived.

What does a man of faith in a control narrative do when an angry God desires to destroy everything with a flood? He faithfully and obediently works night and day on his salvation with one fearful eye always searching the sky; he builds a boat and prays he survives the coming destruction.

I know many believers who serve a God in control; a God they perceive as angry and wrathful; a God who seeks to punish sin with destruction. They work day and night on their salvation. They live fearfully, one eye always searching the sky for signs of humanities impending doom. Their prayer life consists of desperate pleas for a stay of execution. They seek to survive.

Please understand, I am not suggesting Noah got it wrong, in the narrative of his day, he knocked it out of the park! But I am suggesting that if we, today, perceive God through the same control lens Noah did, we will live in the same narrative.

Have you ever wondered why we have a Christian sub-culture in America?

I would like to suggest it's because much of the church still interprets God and man through the lens of sovereign control. Therefore, when it gets darker in the world, Christians don't get brighter; no, they build a sub-culture; they become survivors, looking for a way to navigate the coming flood.

But I would like to suggest that if a flood where prophesied today, building an ark to survive it would be counter to the gospel of Jesus.

We have the whole story! *"...for the Son of Man did not come to destroy men's lives, but to save them."*

Christians aren't called to fear floods; we aren't even called to survive them. We are called to live like Jesus; to release His Kingdom on earth as it is in heaven. We are called to overcome, to break through, to live as expressions of sovereign love.

We have the whole story and in Christ, we can live in such a powerfully surrendered way that floods must bend the knee.

In the revelation of sovereign love, we have been commissioned to reveal salvation to all we encounter, to bring light to every dark place. We are called to release hope to the hopeless, redemption to the prodigal, salvation, transformation and life to every dead, broken and hurting place. We are invited to live confident and sure as powerful expressions of His sovereign love *that none would perish.*

We are living in the whole story. If we are willing to walk away from the ideology of sovereign control and make Jesus, sovereign love, our lens, our hermeneutic, our methodology for interpretation, we will become a church that doesn't fear floods. Instead, floods will fear us.

Please get this, we aren't here to call down fire! Nor are we here to build a Christian sub-culture in which we might survive – a boat for the world-ending flood. *"On earth as it is in heaven,"*[17] that's why we are here. *"Even greater works shall you do."*[18] That's what Jesus revealed and promised.

A Greater Revelation

Noah couldn't do something outside his theology. But more to the point, neither can we.

Sovereign control is the narrowest lens through which to know God. It's salvation through works. It takes the least amount of faith and doesn't take into account God's eternal and sovereign love.

To describe God as sovereignly in control is an earthbound

[17]*See Matthew 6:10*
[18]*See John 14:12*

perspective; it doesn't include heaven's perspective. It is finite thinking dictated by the fear of coming floods. A God in control is human reasoning. While it may seem to be an accurate assessment of our experience, while it may appear true from where we are standing, it's not the truth that sets us free.

Sovereign control is not in God's nature; it's in man's perception. It only works outside the revelation of perfect love and the context of eternity.

We need a better perspective, a greater revelation.

Who Knows the True Color of the Zebra?

There are some profound similarities between Noah and Jesus. Both were righteous men. Both walked in radical obedience. Both lived a powerful faith. Both were mocked and persecuted for their trust in God, and both lived in such a powerful way as to establish a future, a new world for the generations to come.

But their approach to life and ministry and the world around them couldn't have been more different. Why? Because their theology was vastly different.

Noah's theology was control. Noah faithfully obeyed and he and his family survived. It's a good story, a true story.

Jesus' theology was love. Jesus faithfully obeyed and He laid down His life, He died. And then Jesus rose and in His resurrection purchased salvation for all. It's a better story, the whole story.

In Noah's narrative, a handful of people survived. In Jesus narrative, all men and women can be saved.

Which narrative do you want to live in?

Survival is what we get with a theology of control; resurrection life is what we get with a theology of love.

I am not suggesting the Bible lessons learned from Noah's faith aren't truly life changing. It's the word of God; it's true.

I *am* suggesting Noah's lens was not definitive or complete regarding the nature of God.

And I'm suggesting there is one way by which to truly read the whole Bible and one way to truly know God…

The speaker then presented the question to us, "Who is correct regarding the true color of the zebra?" He paused long enough for me to have the thought, "Zebras are white and black."

But that wasn't the question.

"Who knows the true color of the zebra," the speaker asked again and then he answered. "The zebra."

Jesus is the Zebra.

He is sovereign love. He is the whole story. When the Bible is interpreted through Jesus, when our perspective comes into alignment with His, we join in the whole story and we begin to live sure in the power of our salvation, in the power of resurrection life!

chapter seven

THE WHIPPING SWITCH

Now Get

He was a gifted speaker. His style bordered on the theatrical. He ended his message with passionate vehemence in his voice, one hand held high, holding a 5-foot-long switch, the kind used to motivate large animals. "There are no spiritual giants in this room." He said.

My heart broke.

Then he pulled the whipping switch down dramatically, the one he had masterfully used as a prop, the one he had skillfully explained was like the hypothetical whipping switch God uses to get us moving or to keep us in line.

"You have everything you need…" he said, reminding us of how God had already done His part. He paused, letting the implication sink in - we better get our butts in gear. Then, with just the right amount of disdain in his voice, he said, "Now get!"

"Now Get," that was the title of his message. A message I was compelled to endure from the front row of all three services. I was trying to keep a poker face, I was trying not to yell, cry, or be sick.

I was the new Director of Ministries at a church, commissioned by the senior pastors to help shift a culture, to empower the people to lean into a greater revelation of grace and freedom. The guy speaking was the well-loved, 16-year veteran leader within the church. And, for a plethora of reasons, he wasn't interested in this culture shift.

"There are no spiritual giants in this room." His guilty verdict hung in the air like sadness. And it was a direct response to the closing statement I had given from the same pulpit just one Sunday earlier; a message where I had closed with the declaration, "Everyone in this room is a spiritual giant."

God Is in a Good Mood

"God is in a good mood." It's the first thing I said the first time I spoke at that church. It was my introduction to nearly every message thereafter. It's a quote from my hero friend, Bill Johnson, pastor of Bethel Church in Redding California. But many within the church hadn't heard of Bill Johnson and weren't drinking even close to that watering hole. So, when I said it from the pulpit, I said it like it was an original thought. It became one of the phrases I was known for. Thanks, Bill.

Most people like the idea of a God in a good mood; many even believe it's possibly true, at least occasionally. Often when I would run into church members they would ask with an amused twinkle in their eyes, "Is God still in a good mood?"

I would always smile and respond, "He is so happy, it's crazy!" or "He couldn't be more pleased!" or "Oh man, He's in such a stunningly good mood today that you should probably ask Him for something!"

It's an empowering and transformative thought – a happy God. If believed, it can change a life, a family, the world and even a church culture.

A good God in a good mood is the good news; it's the gospel

message. It's what Jesus revealed in His life, death and resurrection. A good Father sent His good Son in the power of His good Holy Spirit to redeem His sons and daughters and restore them to living an infinitely good life as powerfully good children.

Jesus came to redeem what was lost in the fall. He died and rose so we could know our Father's perfect love and discover a transformed life. He came to empower us into righteousness; He said it would look like greater works. In Christ, our identity is secure. We are no longer sinners but saints. We are no longer dwarfed by the sorrows of this world; in Christ, we are spiritual giants.

"Everyone in this room is a spiritual giant."

That's how I closed my message the Sunday prior to the infamous whipping switch sermon. And a week later, as the switch came down, and as I sat dumbfounded; I realized just how different my God lens was from that of my whip-wielding brother.

A Culture of Control

There are two ways to know God, two theologies on the earth today, the theology of *the tree of the knowledge of good and evil* or the theology of *the tree of life.*

One is a theology of control and its fruit is fear and insecurity, the other is a theology of love and its fruit righteousness, peace and joy; one demands obedience and behavior modification, the other empowers obedience and with it, revelation, transformation and access to our redeemed identity in Christ. One reacts *to* life, the other responds *from* life, one restricts, the other sets free and empowers.

Just so, there are two ways to lead people and form culture – seek to control them or seek to empower them. And while both get results, only one approach truly leads to life.

These two approaches are determined by what we believe about God. If we believe God wants control, we will develop a culture of control. If we believe our God wants to empower us in the authority of His sovereign love, we will develop a culture of freedom.

In case his prop wasn't a big enough clue, control is the narrative my whip-wielding brother was developing. You see, in a culture of control, God carries a whipping switch.

If we believe God wants control, we also, consciously or otherwise, believe we need to be controlled. The first belief births the other. They go hand in glove.

A church that believes God wants control is a church that needs to be controlled. A church that believes God is controlling is a church full of people who believe they are prone to wander.

And it gets worse!

A church that believes they are prone to wander is a church whose gospel message is built around behavior modification. And a church focused on behavior eventually becomes a powerless, punishment-focused church, a people better known for what they are against than what they are for. Sound familiar?

And in this powerless church, the leader must promote an angry whipping switch wielding God in order to motivate good behavior lest the people succumb to their propensity to sin. The leader must constantly exhort the people to live righteously while at the same time condemning them to a sinful nature. The message is a paralysis of "try harder" Christianity under the rule of a bi-polar God.

And what's really crazy is, in this culture of control, the people thank the leader for the whipping switch message.

Seriously!

I heard people give feedback on that infamous Sunday that sounded a little like this…

"That was a tough but good word pastor, thanks for knocking me around."

And,

"We both know I am a dirty sinner and, well, who knows what I might do if you weren't here to remind me."

Where do you think the act of Flagellantism came from?

Yeah, I had to look it up too. Flagellantism is the word used to describe when people whip themselves. It is typically connected to 13th and 14th century Catholicism. You have probably seen it portrayed in a movie – a fella strips his shirt off, falls to his knees, takes a braded tasseled whip and slings it over his shoulder and against his back until he is bruised and bloodied.

And let's face it, when you watched it; you knew it represented brokenness - a flawed way of thinking. It painted God as a demanding brute.

And yet the spirit of Flagellantism is sadly alive and well in the church and therefore the world. So much so that many thank the pastor when he is abusive.

The extent to which we believe in the controlling-God narrative is the extent to which we believe we must be whipped and… "Why thank you pastor, I was having a hard time reaching that spot."

My point: if God wants control, then the goal of leadership within the church is also control. And then the goal of the people in the church is control, and then the goal within marriage is control, and the goal of parenting is control, in friendship, in business, in neighborhood communities, in government... the generations become enslaved to a behavior-based mindset, a control narrative.

The control narrative does not lead to life and it is not the Kingdom Jesus revealed. But if we insist to live with a theology of control we will find ourselves in a prison of our own making.

A Prison of Our Own Making

The fact is, all humanity is born into a prison system, a punitive control-based reality. Guilty and prone to wander, we lived imprisoned to our own lusts and the enemy of our soul.

But when we surrender to Jesus, when we repent, we are forgiven of our sins. Truly and fully. And with that forgiveness comes salvation. Salvation from our past, and also salvation so we can live a righteous future - like spiritual giants.

While we were born into a prison system, Jesus set us free!

Sadly, a theology of control actually undermines our access to that freedom. It withholds from us the empowering grace by which to live from our redeemed identity in Christ. You see, the theology of control propagates the belief that, even after salvation, we are still prone to wander.

A sinner inherently believes they shouldn't have freedom because they inherently believe they wouldn't be trustworthy with it.

My point? A theology of control becomes a prison of our own making in which we assign God the role of Warden and we take the role of the sinner perpetually needing to be regulated.

In this prison of our own making, we place our faith in the ideology of a Warden god. He takes care of us, He makes sure we get a cot, three meals a day and an hour in the yard. Just enough.

We also make the Warden god responsible to keep us in line. In fact, he becomes responsible for every aspect of our lives, thus removing us from all responsibility. Then, when we can't control ourselves, we imagine the whipping switch in the Wardens hand. Why? Because we deserve it.

In our little finite narrative, the Warden is so wonderful at noting our failures and weaknesses; he won't let us get away with anything.

In this prison culture, if we mess up, the Warden has some of the other prisoners beat us to teach us a lesson. And of course, sometimes, on behalf of the Warden, we are the ones giving the lessons. We call it, "tough love."

But it's not love, it's a perversion birthed from the narrative of control. It's a prison of our own making.

A theology where God is sovereignly in control is also a theology where Christians live cut off from the ability to control themselves.

The control narrative disempowers and imprisons saints in a daily wrestling match with a proclivity to sin. They are unable to do anything of Kingdom significance because all of their focus and energy goes into trying to survive the day without sinning.

But Jesus gave us the whole story and it wasn't about control, it was about freedom discovered in the authority of love.

Authority vs. Control

"Then Jesus came to them and said, *"All authority in heaven and on earth has been given to me."*[1] Jesus didn't say, *"all control"* He said, *"all authority."*

The funny thing about control and authority is they can often look the same and may even appear to yield the same results, but they are actually in direct opposition with each other. Authority will never seek control and control never operates from true authority. They are two opposing mindsets, two conflicting narratives.

Jesus explains this in Matthew 7:22-23 *"Many will say to me on that day, 'Lord, Lord, did we not prophesy in your name and in your name drive out demons and in your name perform many miracles?' Then I will tell them plainly, 'I never knew you. Away from me, you evildoers!'"*

Jesus is essentially saying, "Hey, you might be doing all the right stuff, you might be operating in power, but I don't know you."

My point? It is entirely possible to do all the right stuff from the wrong narrative. It's actually quite incredible what a person can achieve with a theology of control. But Jesus is clear; He will not acknowledge the results and worse, there will be no intimacy, *"I never knew you."*

Love is not about performance, or achievement. Love is about

---

[1]*Matthew 28:18,* NIV

being known and knowing. If we are living outside of intimacy, we are completely missing the point.

"If I speak in the tongues of men or of angels, but do not have love, I am only a resounding gong or a clanging cymbal. If I have the gift of prophecy and can fathom all mysteries and all knowledge, and if I have a faith that can move mountains, but do not have love, I am nothing. If I give all I possess to the poor and give over my body to hardship that I may boast, but do not have love, I gain nothing."[2]

Paul, in his first letter to the Corinthian church, confirms what Jesus taught. We can do all the right stuff, the things many perceive to be signs of holiness; we can live a structured and principled life, we can achieve much, see powerful results, and yet operate completely outside of the authority of intimacy and completely miss Him.

To be *known* by God is what every one of us is designed for. And to be known by God is to live free, sure in the authority of His love, as love. Anything else is hypocrisy; a performance that will cut us off from being known and knowing; from intimacy.

Not a Counseling Session

I sat across from the couple trying not to fidget, trying to keep a look of calm on my face, I was supposed to be the fella with the answers, the counselor. I wasn't *a* Counselor.

I'd considered becoming *a* Counselor after Bible college. Karen thought I'd be good at it. But when I realized how much more schooling I would need, I decided against counseling as a full-time profession.

Years later, I became *a* family pastor. Yes, it *is* funny.

When the couple asked to meet with me, it was simply to, "talk through some communication issues." The wife felt like she wasn't always heard and the husband wanted to "do better." I had the impression it would be a lighthearted session.

And it was. And then it wasn't.

---

[2] *1 Corinthians 13:1-3*, NIV

Everything was going great. We talked about love languages. We discussed carving out intentional time together. We navigated some of their parenting tensions. And after each subject, I would begin to conclude the meeting only to hear myself say, "I sense there's more."

It was starting to feel awkward, especially after the wife asked me what I meant by "more" and I didn't know.

As a non-counselor in a counseling situation, I was simply doing the only thing I was truly qualified to do; follow the prompting of the still small voice of Holy Spirit. But it seemed to be causing some discomfort for all involved. Have you ever noticed how following the Comforter is often uncomfortable?

There was a definite tension in the room.

I finally decided to ease the disquiet by closing our time in prayer when suddenly the husband started weeping. Then, to his wife's and my surprise, he began to describe the affairs he'd been having over the last several years.

"Oh, that's what, 'there's more' meant" I thought as I sat trying not to fidget, trying to keep a look of calm on my face.

To be honest, I was a little overwhelmed. It was ugly, sad, and heart breaking; his last several years had been *"a living hell."* And this hell had been crushing this husband for years; and now it was crushing his wife. This hell had oppressed, lied, controlled, demanded, accused. This hell had been marked by shame, condemnation, despair, separation and sorrow - so much sorrow.

This man had been living in a prison of his own making. He went to church, he tithed, he provided for his family and he was an upstanding member of the community. He was doing all the right stuff, but there was no intimacy. And he wanted so very much to be free.

I learned long before I was a family pastor who wasn't *a* Counselor that I have one responsibility in every session; no matter the carnage, no matter the hell, no matter the bondage, I am the person with hope.

You see, years earlier I had learned that sovereign Love is greater than every broken experience on the planet. Love can redeem every tragedy. Every horror, every "living hell" can be worked to good.

While I sat listening, and a little overwhelmed, I reminded myself over and again, *"Love is bigger. Love can redeem this mess. Love is more powerful. Love can forgive, set free, love can heal and restore and save this couple, their family, the legacy they were designed to live and leave. Love is sovereign. Love has all authority!"*

The Authority of Love

When truth comes face to face with a lie, it doesn't control the lie, the lie is simply exposed and no longer has power to control. That's why truth sets us free. When light shines, there is simply no more darkness. And it's not some great battle... truth and light don't have to do push-ups. It's simply the nature of truth to expose a lie; it's simply the nature of light to dispel darkness.

You see, it's not in truth's nature to control, it's not in light's nature to control, and it's not in love's nature to control.

Authority is simply truth being revealed and light shining. Authority is simply perfect love being sovereign.

Jesus showed us that the controls of this fallen world couldn't exist in the same space as the authority and power of sovereign love. Lepers were healed, storms were calmed, demons cast out, and above all, relationships were restored.

Where the authority of sovereign Love *is*, every controlling fear *isn't*. Love *is* and poverty *isn't*. Love *is* and sickness *isn't*. Love *is* and greed *isn't*. Love *is* and insecurity *isn't*. Love *is* and hatred *isn't*.

And for the couple whose marriage was on shaky ground, where Love *is*, shame, condemnation, rejection, broken trust, despair, separation and sorrow *isn't*.

Love, sovereign Love, walks powerfully into every controlling broken narrative and our "living hell" bends the knee.

And here is where it gets amazing, God has invited *us* to live in the same authority and power of sovereign love by faith. He has invited us to live in that same heaven-to-earth narrative.

"All authority in heaven and on earth has been given to me. Therefore go…"[3]

Jesus has all authority and He gave it to us. All the authority of His sovereign love, it's been given through Christ to sons and daughters.

It's the same authority Jesus displayed when He healed the sick, the lame, the blind. It's the same authority Jesus revealed when He fed thousands and challenged religious hypocrisy.

We are called to know and live in the same authority Jesus knew and revealed. We are to be a living revelation of hope. And when we live in the intimate authority of love, people are set free.

Not a Counseling Session, Continued…

While I sat listening, and a little overwhelmed, I reminded myself over and again, *"Love is bigger. Love is sovereign. Love has all authority!"*

And then, over the next hour and a half, I spoke the measureless revelation of love over them. I gave them access to the whole story. With every word, I released grace. At every turn, I revealed hope. Holy Spirit was with me, Wisdom a close friend. And the authority and power of sovereign Love began to transform the atmosphere in the room.

Yes, there was a deep sadness, but the authority of Love was greater still as light invaded darkness. Hearts softened and the truth of heavens perspective began to set free.

I witnessed sincere repentance by the husband; the work of forgiveness in his wife, and then true powerful hope and the beginning of restoration.

[3]*Matthew 28:18-19,* NIV

I sat in awe as the couple held each other weeping while recommitting one to another. Their tears the testimony of sorrow and joy, evidence of the power of resurrection life.

They laughed as they embraced - sovereign Love had begun the glorious work of transformation. It was intimate, joyous and holy. It was a beautiful miracle.

Yes, there was a road ahead of them - a continued journey of choosing surrender, and forgiveness and trust. But what we experienced over the course of nearly two and a half hours was unbelievable; the power of sovereign Love redeeming the past and restoring the future; the wonder of sovereign Love saving a lost couple from a living hell. God's always good love was setting them free.

Here's what I am convinced is true. If I had navigated that critical moment, when the husband broke down, with a theology of control, I may have achieved results, but intimacy would not have been one of them.

While a whipping switch may seem appropriate for this situation, I believe it would have been destructive to the future of their marriage.

Only the power and authority of sovereign Love could restore this marriage. Only a God in a good mood could save them.

Not once did I identify the husband with his behavior. I treated him like a spiritual giant who had desperately missed the mark. I called him into his identify. Understand, I didn't white wash what he had done. We went at it straight on, the broken, ugly, mess that he had made. This was uncompromising Love, a forceful encounter with the power of mercy and grace.

And not once did I identify the wife with her experience as a victim. I treated her as a spiritual giant who could powerfully choose to forgive and restore. I called her into her identity. Understand, I didn't ignore her pain and fractured trust. We went at it straight on, the broken, ugly, mess that he had made. This was sovereign Love, a gentle encounter with the power of mercy and grace.

Here's the deal, a whipping switch is about punishment and performance. It would have identified the wife with her pain and the husband with his guilt and shame. The only way forward would have been a husband seeking redemption through acts of Flagellantism and a wife feeling safe only when she was in control. Their marriage would become a prison of their own making.

The whole point of marriage is intimacy and a whipping switch might as well be a gun...

A Church that Changes the World

Jesus revealed sovereign love and it had nothing to do with the clanging cymbals of control. He endured the ugly horror of the whipping switch. He experienced the shame of the control narrative and He scorned it. He held it with contempt and disdain. And He died and rose so we could be free from the prison of punishment and performance.

What we believe about God's nature determines what we believe about everything else. Men and women controlled by an occasionally irritated and even angry God who carries a whipping switch, are men and women dwarfed by a perceived sinful nature. Men and women dwarfed by a sinful nature are men and women who don't live like Jesus lived.

But the revelation of Jesus as an always good, always perfect love, empowers us into trust and intimacy; it releases mercy and grace for redemption and transformation. The surer we are regarding the goodness of God, the surer we live as His sons and daughters revealing and releasing His goodness, the gospel.

Suddenly we aren't focused on behavior, we aren't dwarfed by shame or pain: instead, we are a body of believers leaning into intimacy. Suddenly we are spiritual giants; in our marriages, in our parenting, in our friendships, in every relationship and area of influence, we are growing sure in the authority and power of sovereign love.

And a body of believers sure in love is a church that changes the world.

chapter eight

HEAVEN AND HELL

Introduction

The moment I started suggesting that God's sovereignty is not defined by control is the moment I met some angry people who felt they must challenge the idea.

Their proof? Hell.

Heaven

The best way to expose a lie is to be immersed in the truth. The best way to illuminate darkness is to have a very bright light.

In the same way, I would like to suggest that the best way to perceive hell is through a greater revelation of the Kingdom of heaven.

Jesus gave us our focus and our mandate when He taught us to pray, "*Thy Kingdom come, on earth as it is in heaven.*"[1] And Jesus lived as an

---

[1]*See Matthew 6:10 KJV*

expression of that Kingdom, "*that He might destroy the works of the devil.*"[2]

I would like to suggest that any thought about hell that isn't interpreted through the measureless revelation of heaven should be held suspect; any conclusion about hell that isn't birthed from sovereign love is flawed and therefore dangerous to our spiritual and emotional well-being.

I have found that those who tend to preach most fervently on the horrors of hell and eternal damnation seem to have very little evidence of the Kingdom of heaven in their lives. You know, the *righteousness, peace and joy in the Holy Spirit* that Paul wrote about in Romans 14:17. Those last two evidences, *peace* and *joy*? They are often markedly absent.

Everything Jesus said and did, both established the Kingdom of heaven, and destroyed anything that resembled hell – the works of the devil.

And so, in this chapter, as you read some of my thoughts on hell, here are a handful of things it would be helpful for you to know.

First, my passion and focus is to establish His Kingdom on earth as it is in heaven thus destroying the works of the enemy.

Second, I am a relational theologian who has written a book on the goodness of God that highlights the disparity between control and love. I have done this all to empower a greater trust and intimacy with God. The focus and intent for this chapter is no different.

Third, I am aware of the contentious climate around the subject of hell within much of the North American church today. My thoughts are not definitive. Please take them as suggestions from a fellow traveler and let not your heart be troubled.

Fourth, this chapter is not an attempt to convince people on whether hell exists or not. It does. This chapter is about looking at hell through the sovereignty of love so we may confidently fulfill our mandate to establish His Kingdom and destroy the works of the enemy.

---

[2]*See 1 John 3:8 KJV*

Ultimately, this chapter is an attempt to expose how a theology of sovereign control has distorted our understanding regarding the nature of God and His relationship to humanity, particularly when it comes to how we, the church, have most recently defined and navigated the reality of hell.

Twist the Knife

Many years ago, I had lunch with a wealthy Christian businessman. Karen and I had just launched our ministry, A Family Story.[3] This fella, endeavoring to be helpful, explained his business model as a way to instruct us on how to develop our ministry model.

"Jason, do you know how you lead someone to God?" He asked rhetorically before continuing.

"You find where they have been wounded..." while talking, he leaned toward me and began poking at my bicep insinuating a gaping laceration, "...you make them painfully aware of the hell they are experiencing in their life. "You poke and prod at the wound..." He poked and prodded at my arm... "until they are fully and painfully aware of their desperate circumstance."

I winced in horror. This was exactly the response he was looking for. His eyes lit up and he continued.

"Then you take a knife..." he made a fist as if he held the weapon in his hand, picture an 8-inch serrated bowie knife, "...and you thrust!" He demonstrated with a forceful stabbing motion against my imaginary wound.

"Then, when the knife is in the cut," He paused for affect, "You twist the blade!" He turned his fist violently against my arm.

Still misunderstanding my horrified grimace, He sat back, crossed his arms and nodded with satisfaction, "Finally, when they are in agony and can't take it anymore, you give them their salvation, the answer, Jesus."

---

[3] *www.afamilystory.org*

Sadly, most of the Western world, at some point in their lives, have experienced this man's ministry model. The reason they have is because it works… if the goal is to get someone to buy a product or recite a prayer.

The problem, however, is obvious. It's spiritual manipulation. And it has devastating consequences. A god who manipulates our pain, who enhances our awareness of shame and brokenness so He can gain our trust, is a god who cannot be trusted.

I once saw a cartoon that illustrates the problem well. Jesus was knocking on a door and from inside came the response,

"Who's there"

"Jesus, I'm here to save you."

"From what?"

"From what I'll do to you if you don't let me in."

That cartoon, and its attempt at humor, unfortunately reflects the heartbreaking perspective much of the Western church has on God, hell and salvation. For centuries, this perspective of hell has been used as an evangelistic tool. "Turn or burn" has defined much of Christian colloquialism for far too long!

I believe this type of ministry model is birthed directly from a theology of sovereign control. You see, sovereign control leads to a punitive perspective of Hell; they go hand in glove. A control narrative needs an ultimate punishment scenario or it doesn't work. A controlling God will use the fear and pain of hell to manipulate us into choosing heaven.

But the idea that God might control and manipulate our pain so we might be saved is not just devastating, it's blackmail…

Pain

As the famous atheist Christopher Hitchens once said, "Hell is blackmail."

For centuries now, much of the Western church has presented hell through the lens of sovereign control. And Atheism is its purest by-product.

Atheism is the most intellectually honest response to the disparate idea of a good God who wants to save us from the hell He will send us to if we don't give Him control.

When Atheists defend their position, they reveal what they believe about the god they claim doesn't exist; He is a controlling disinterested monster, a harsh master who expects us to give him his due while never concerning himself with our pain.

Pain, that's the foundation of Atheism.

Actually, pain is the foundation of all false religions.

Pain, experienced through poverty, war, abuse, racism, sickness, violence, natural disasters, a sense of separation...

To Atheists, pain is the proof that hell exists.

It's a bit ironic, but you could say that the Atheist's argument that God does not exist is firmly based in their certainty regarding the existence of hell. Not some afterlife hell, the living hell that can be tasted and touched here and now.

For those with a theology of sovereign control, the existence of hell here on earth is the foundational argument that there is no God. It's a good argument too, because while God may be harder to prove in a control narrative, hell is as plain as the nose on your face; hell, well, it most certainly exists.

You don't have to search hard to find evidence. It looks like the sex trade, child slavery, the homeless widow and orphan, divorce, the hopeless feeling that there is no other option but abortion, or suicide. It looks like cancer, or crippling depression, sickness, loneliness and suffering. It looks like the destruction caused by the tsunami...

The Atheist chooses Atheism because it's less painful than the idea that love is somehow defined by a good God sovereignly in control of such devastation. Atheists choose Atheism because in a control narrative, it's too painful not to.

But what if God is not about control and therefore hell is not about punishment? What if hell could be perceived another way? What if sovereign love revealed the whole story?

The Parable of the Talents

There was a master with three servants. He was going on a journey and he called the servants to himself and gave each of them a gift. *"To one he gave five talents (of money), to another two talents, and to another one talent, each according to his own ability. Then he went on his journey."*[4]

You probably know this story. It's found in Matthew 25 and told by Jesus. Among other things, this is a parable about heaven and hell.

Eventually the master returns home to, as Jesus put it, *"Settle accounts with them."* Jesus doesn't tell us how, but the first two servants doubled what they had been given and both received a, *"Well done, good and faithful servant! You have been faithful with a few things; I will put you in charge of many things. Come and share your master's happiness!"*[5]

But the last servant, it didn't go so well for him. When he came before the master, he said something heartbreaking and revealing: *"Master, I knew you to be a harsh and hard man, reaping where you did not sow, and gathering where you had not scattered seed. So I was afraid, and I went and hid your talent in the ground. Here you have what is your own."*[5]

The unfaithful servant believed a lie about the nature of the master – he perceived the master as unjust and untrustworthy.

And so, the servant rejected the gift the master had given him. *"Have what is your own,"* he said and he returned the one talent.

This servant didn't get a well done. *"His master replied, 'You wicked, lazy servant! So, you knew that I harvest where I have not sown and gather where I have not scattered seed?'"*[6]

---

[4] *Matthew 25:15*, ESV
[5] *See Matthew 25:21*, NIV
[6] *Matthew 25:24-25*, NIV

It was a question, not a declaration. The master was challenging the deception of the unfaithful servants' premise.

Then, after telling the servant that at the very least he could have banked the money for interest, the master makes a statement that seems to prove the unfaithful servant's thoughts about him true: *"Throw that worthless servant outside, into the darkness, where there will be weeping and gnashing of teeth."*[7]

I would like to suggest that if we believe a lie about the goodness of God, eventually we will experience a hell that seems to prove the lie true.

This story reveals something powerfully important, we reap the narrative that we sow into.

Neither Death nor Life

"For I am convinced that neither death nor life, neither angels nor demons, neither the present nor the future, nor any powers, neither height nor depth, nor anything else in all creation, will be able to separate us from the love of God that is in Christ Jesus our Lord."[8]

Paul reveals in this scripture that Love is sovereign; that there is no place that Love does not exist, nowhere Love does not have all authority and nothing more powerful than Love. And this is true in life and in death.

David wrote it this way. *"Where can I go from your Spirit? Where can I flee from your presence? If I go up to the heavens, you are there; if I make my bed in the depths (in death), you are there."*[9]

While I am absolutely convinced that we can feel separated from God, I am equally convinced it's never on His end.

My point? While we can never escape His love; we can reject it, while He is light, we can choose darkness, while He is always the truth, we can choose to believe a lie.

While many would suggest that hell is the separation from God's

---

[7]*Matthew 25:30*, NIV
[8]*Romans 8:38-39*, NIV
[9]*Psalms 139:7-8*, NIV

love, I would like to suggest that hell is the stubborn rejection of God's love. Hell is not the absence of love, Hell is the denial and refusal of the perfect goodness of God's love.

The Parable of the Talents Continued...

Have you ever wondered why the unfaithful servant only received one talent where the others received multiple?

I would like to propose that the one talent was an act of kindness by a good master. You see, the unfaithful servant perceived the master as, *"a harsh and hard man, reaping where (he) did not sow, and gathering where (he) had not scattered seed."*

Can you imagine what it would be like to be given a sum of money from someone you believe is looking for opportunities to punish you; an unjust and controlling master who is always looking for opportunities to twist the knife?

Because of how the unfaithful servant perceived his master, he didn't receive the one talent as a blessing; he saw it as a burden. The gift wasn't a sign of favor; it was simply further proof of the master's cruelty.

Jesus told us how this can happen in our lives when He said, *"The eye is the lamp of the body. If your eyes are healthy, your whole body will be full of light. But if your eyes are unhealthy, your whole body will be full of darkness. If then the light within you is darkness, how great is that darkness!"*[10]

Essentially, the blessing of the talent that the master gave to the unfaithful servant was perceived through unhealthy eyes as a curse. When generosity is perceived as cruelty, when love is perceived as hate, when light is perceived as darkness, *how great is that darkness!*

The unfaithful servant hid the talent, and not just anywhere. He was so paranoid, so terrified that he couldn't even trust a bank. Can you picture it? The servant out in the deep of night in a mad frenzy of fear, digging a hole and burying the talent where only he could find it?

---

[10] *Matthew 6:22-23,* NIV

Imagine how he suffered daily.

Imagine how his family suffered as well - impoverished, insecure, broken hearted. When they faced financial hardship, an economic meltdown, a fiscal emergency, they had to stay vigilant, they had to defend the talent above all else.

The unfaithful servant spent all his energy on not spending the talent. His focus was on what he couldn't do. He was behavior-driven in a control narrative, a sinner in the hands of an angry God. His life was a list of dont's. His days and nights were spent in a neurosis of mistrust. He was focused on not losing the talent like a sinner is focused on the horrors of hell.

The good gift given by a good master became his prison, his suffocation, his living hell. Because the unfaithful servant believed a lie about the unjust controlling nature of his master, he experienced hell long before the master returned and confirmed it.

The fact is, what we perceive determines what we believe, our ability to trust, and the entire trajectory of our life.

What We Perceive

Everything is a matter of perspective. If we perceive light through unhealthy eyes, we will see darkness. If we perceive truth through unhealthy eyes, we will see lies. God is love and His love is sovereign, but if we see love through the lens of control, we will experience striving and desperation.

The three servants had very different experiences even though they all received the same gift. The first two thrived while the third suffered. The faithful servants perceived the master to be faithful and received the talents as blessing and opportunity. The unfaithful servant perceived the master as faithless and rejected the talent as a curse.

If we perceive God as a harsh controlling master, then our interactions with Him will prove He is a harsh and controlling master. And then everything that happens, every interaction with our fellow man, supports that harsh control narrative. And then everything we read in the Bible enforces His control. Control becomes our gospel, our supreme reality.

Then our Christian religion is about control; our ideology is about control, our history books and our future, all about control.

And then of course hell becomes our ultimate proof of His control.

The fact is, the world perceives hell solely through the lens of sovereign control. It is a destination to be feared, an eternal punishment for those who wouldn't let God control their lives. Sadly, many believers perceive hell the same way. As though it's a destination to be feared instead of an experience to be redeemed and a reality to be defeated here on earth.

Sovereign Control and Hell

Like Jesus, our mandate is to establish God's Kingdom on earth as it is in heaven and in so doing, destroy the works of the devil.

And, as you may have guessed, eight chapters into this book, I would like to suggest that the first work of the devil that must be destroyed is the pernicious lie of sovereign control. I suggest this because the lie of sovereign control was the first and foundational work of the devil here on earth. The control perspective was introduced by a snake in the garden and Adam and Eve believed it.

And the moment Adam and Eve bought into the lie sovereign control is the moment humanity was positioned in the insecure reality of the existence of hell. Suddenly they were naked and ashamed. And they hid from God.

Suddenly their perception regarding the goodness of God was distorted and *how great was that darkness!*

Sovereign control was the first lie that sought to separate humanity from the intimacy of sovereign love. I would like to suggest that the theology of sovereign control is actually what introduced hell into the human experience.

The Parable of the Talents Continued...

Sovereign love was the narrative Jesus revealed in everything He did and in every story He told, including the parable of the talents; a parable that revealed God's perspective on heaven and on hell.

The faithful servants were those who perceived the true nature of the master—that he was good. This set them free to trust, which empowered them to receive and invest the master's good gift. They lived in the present toward a glorious future.

While Jesus didn't tell us what the faithful servants did to double their talents, He did describe their reward— *"Well done, good and faithful servant...come and share your master's happiness."* The faithful servants simply continued in the trajectory of their faith - *heaven.*

The unfaithful servant was the one who perceived the nature of the master to be evil – he rejected the masters good gift. His perception undermined trust and he lived desperate and afraid.

Jesus did tell us what this servant did. He buried the talent, not even investing it in a bank. He lived *wicked and lazy* toward a hopeless future. The unfaithful servant simply continued in the trajectory of his unbelief – hell.

In this chapter, you may have noticed that I underlined the words faithful and unfaithful. I did this to highlight the role of faith in a servant's perception.

Faith believes God is always good. Faith is expressed through choosing to trust in the sovereign love of God. Faithfulness establishes His Kingdom on earth as it is in heaven. The faithful experience righteousness, peace and joy in the Holy Spirit, they live increasingly aware of the power and evidence of their reward, a *well done* – heaven.

Unbelief is the denial and rejection of the sovereign love of God. The faithless live desperate and afraid, they suffer and are increasingly convinced in the power and evidence of hell.

The power of faith—that's what Jesus was revealing in the parable of the talents. But it wasn't faith in what to do, it was faith regarding how we will perceive.

Where the eye is single, the body is full of light...

Hell and Salvation

I asked Jesus into my heart when I was five. And in my hazy collection of five-year-old memories, that moment stands out vivid and powerful - the family room of our house on Russell St, the 1970's burnt orange and forest green flowered couch, the maple coffee table I knelt at as my mom led me in the sinner's prayer.

I felt God's love and goodness like laughter, I knew His affection, I sensed His great pleasure. And even at that young and innocent age, I had a sense of being made new.

Like everyone on the planet, I was born into the first Adam, I was guilty and insecure. When I was reborn into the second Adam, Jesus redeemed and made me whole. And I knew it. Even at five years old, growing up with parents that loved God and others well, having never truly experienced the ravages of sin, when I said yes to Jesus, I still felt powerfully the joy of being forgiven.

Even though, at my young age, I didn't truly understand sin, I felt its sense of separation. And in Jesus, I knew I was saved and beautifully included.

My point? I didn't need a lesson in pain and the popular teaching of hell to desire Jesus in my life; I didn't need an 8-inch serrated bowie knife to provoke repentance. I didn't need to meet Satan and all his friends in order to desire to know and revel in God's good love.

When I asked Jesus to come into my heart, I had absolutely no framework for the concept of hell that is propagated by the control narrative. The punitive idea of hell was foreign to me\ as it should be to all five year olds; as it should be to all of us, regardless of our age... *"Unless we change and become like a little child..."*[11]

---

[11]*See Matthew 18:3*, NIV

The fact is, I was drawn to Jesus that day for one reason; my parents had revealed His love and kindness and I wanted to know Him like they knew Him.

I was safe and loved. And in that stunning context, I desired a personal relationship with Jesus.

All salvation experiences are miraculous and beautiful. There isn't one more stunning than the next. But I don't know anyone who wouldn't trade a lifetime of the insecurity of sin for an opportunity to know Jesus from the beginning.

I am eternally grateful that I was given that opportunity. But I shared my salvation story with you for a reason. You see, I know from experience that it is possible to desire God without even the slightest comprehension of eternal punishment.

My point? Hell has been misrepresented by much of the church for so long that for many it's become a core tenet of the Christian faith. As though we are saved both by grace through faith in Christ *and* by our belief in the power of eternal punishment.

The idea that eternal punishment plays any role in our salvation or faith life is flawed. When it comes to hell, our only responsibility is to destroy the works of the devil and establish heaven.

Conclusion

It is my passion to become so sure in sovereign love that at the end of my life I am not shocked by how good heaven is. Why? Because I am simply following the trajectory of my faith. I believe it is possible to live always in a greater revelation of His Kingdom.

My point? I am not waiting to get to heaven to learn about heaven. While heaven is infinitely better than I "*can ask, or imagine,*"[12] I am getting a head start on asking and imagining it here and now. I am stewarding my faith in sovereign Love and in so doing, I am destroying the works of the devil.

---

[12]*See Ephesians 3:20*

My focus is heaven not hell. And I imagine there will be some disappointed by that. I imagine there will be some who will open this book, go directly to this chapter and read it solely to know what I believe about eternal suffering.

And they will have completely missed my point.

You see, I'm convinced that as son of God, it's not my job to prove hell, it's my job to reveal heaven.

chapter nine

IT'S A TRAP!

The Rules of Being Interviewed

My first rule for being interviewed - *Don't wear plaid.*

It was a new experience for me, being interviewed for television. My first book had just released and to help promote it, my publisher had set them up, radio, print and TV interviews.

I sat nervous on an uncomfortable couch as a fella clipped and then tucked a lapel mic just inside the collar of my button down plaid shirt.

"That's a great plaid shirt," my interviewer said. She was smiling as if she knew a secret.

I was too much the rookie to know you shouldn't wear plaid on camera unless you layer it with a sweater or jacket. Or you are acting in a Highlander movie. *"Small repetitive patterns like pinstripes, chevron, plaid, and houndstooth are difficult to see on video and can make your viewers dizzy." From Dressing for Camera by Alice Currier*

"Thanks," I said. It was my favorite plaid shirt.

She gave a knowing smile to the makeup lady who was applying cover-up to my face. The makeup lady returned her smile and that's when I suspected I was missing something.

Did I mention there was a makeup lady?

This leads to my second rule of being interviewed – *Too much cover up makes you look like an Oompa Loompa. Feel free to say, "I'm good, thanks."*

The cameras started rolling...

Did you know most interviews are scripted? I didn't. When Jimmy Fallon asked Matt Damon if he had done anything crazy lately, He already knew Matt was going to knock it out of the park with a killer African safari story that included bouncing across Kruger National Park in an open Land Rover, a bizarre night of baboon babble, and an encounter with a rabid rhinoceros.

Our interview was not scripted. Which leads to my third rule of being interviewed - *Scripted is better, at least, for beginners.*

Her first question was easy; I know the names of my wife and kids by heart. But the second question was a zinger. "Why did you write this book?" she asked all innocent.

For some unknown reason, I hadn't prepared for that question.

Suddenly I couldn't remember my wife's name let alone why I had written the book; something about God, and my life's message, and a story about my dog. I said some words that resembled sentences until I felt I'd talked long enough.

There was panic in my eyes by then, but my interviewer was a pro. She changed her approach; her questions became leading, and to obvious conclusions. You know, the kind you ask a small child. "Is that ice cream good?"

I started knocking them out of the park, just like Matt Damon.

Then she asked me a question I didn't understand. I literally wasn't sure what she was asking me.

This leads to my fourth rule of being interviewed; a very important rule if you prefer to not look like a bumbling idiot… - *Don't try to answer a question if you literally don't understand the question.*

Yes, I had much to learn. But I've had many interviews since; they have gotten easier. Mostly because years ago God gave me a foundational approach to everything I do and I began applying it to all areas of life, including interviews. It's become the guidepost for all the other rules – *I am not here for me, I'm here to love you.*

Applied to an interview, it goes something like this - *I'm not interviewing to promote myself, a book, an album, or a film. I am interviewing to reveal the perfection of my Father's love.*

This rule helps when I find myself asked unscripted questions, or when I forget and wear plaid again, or when the interviewer isn't a pro.

And it especially helps when the interviewer is hostile.

Didn't I mention? Sometimes the interviewer doesn't like you or what you believe.

Which leads to my fifth rule for being interviewed - *Sometimes the question is a trap. You don't have to answer it, at least not in the way it was asked…*

The trap question is not asked from a sincere desire to hear the answer, but as an attempt to ambush and thereby sabotage the interviewee and their message. The trap question is always asked from a flawed premise and presented in such a way as to force the interviewee to validate the flawed premise.

Often, the question is confrontational and demanding. It will attempt to position you in insecurity. It is asked to set up a basis by which to bring accusation.

You will feel great pressure to answer this question. And you will feel as though there are no good answers, no good options.

Don't answer this question! At least, not the way it was asked. There is a better way...

The Trap Question

There is a story in John 8:1-11 about a woman caught in adultery. There was a man too, but because this happened in a religious control based, male centric culture, it's the woman who's exploited and condemned.

Literally ripped naked from the bed, she was half chased, half dragged through the streets by angry idiots with rocks. They meant to hurtle them at the woman until her bones were broken and her flesh a bloody pulp. They meant to kill her for her sins. It's what she deserved! It's what the narrative of control demands!

Then Jesus, in all the Father's splendor, is thrust into the middle of the story. The woman, weeping and afraid, is flung before Him. Then yanked to her feet, she's forced to stand.

Naked and ashamed, she won't meet His eyes; the feeling of condemnation is so great. Damned, she waits for her punishment. She is guilty. She knows it, the angry mob knows it, even the disciples know it.

"The law says she should be stoned," the men scream, frothing at the mouth. "Our theology of control demands it!"

And then came the trap question.

"Now what do you say? They were using this question as a trap, in order to have a basis for accusing him."[1]

And here's where it gets amazing; Jesus didn't answer the question, at least, not the way it was asked.

Why, because the premise was flawed. The question was not asked from a sincere desire to know the answer, but as an attempt to ambush and sabotage Jesus' message.

The question was asked from the narrative of control.

---

[1]*John 8:5-6,* NIV

Jesus had come to change the lens, to reveal all authority, a new narrative, sovereign Love.

To answer the question the way it was posed would have validated the ugly controlling God narrative. To answer the question would have forced Jesus to either promote murder or endorse adultery; to either pick up a rock and throw it at the woman until she was dead, or leave her in her brokenness and shame.

The theology of sovereign control is a trap. It will always force us to choose between two bondages. But it was for freedom Jesus came, to set us free.[2]

To Set Us Free

We have all felt the ambush of the trap question. We have all experienced the horrible feeling of being forced to either pick up the rock and throw it at the sinner or normalize brokenness.

That's what a theology of control does; it strong-arms us into one of two horribly flawed options; neither of which leads to life and wholeness and freedom; neither of which release mercy and grace.

Because we have embraced a theology of control, the church has been forced to choose between one of two options, throw rocks or endorse sin. It shows up notably today in discussions around homosexuality.

For many years, much of the church answered the question of homosexuality by choosing the horrific first option, throw rocks. And many are still trapped in that bondage.

In recent years, much of the church has chosen the empathetically destructive second option, endorse and even promote homosexuality as God's idea. There is no freedom in that choice either.

Regardless of the sin, a theology of sovereign control will always position Christians into two horrifying insecurities, throw the rock of shame, and condemnation, and fear and hate, or pretend the sin is a part of our nature, make room for its perversion of the truth and develop a

---

[2] *See Galatians 5:1*

culture to support it.

The theology of sovereign control leads to an impotent church known for what it's against, or an impotent church watering down truth until it has no power to set free. Either way, it's an impotent church.

The point? A theology of sovereign control leads us into bondage–either to self-righteous religious activity or to a proclivity to wander.

But Jesus came to set us free. He showed us how to navigate the trap question by how He interacted with both the murderous rock holding mob and the woman caught in her shame and brokenness.

"If any one of you is without sin, let him be the first to throw a stone at her"[3]

Jesus wasn't interested in defending a control narrative. He had one mandate; reveal His Fathers sovereign love. And when sovereign love was revealed, it confronted the heart condition of the murderous mob.

"At this, those who heard began to go away one at a time, the older ones first, until only Jesus was left, with the woman still standing there..." (3)

Jesus would not endorse the control paradigm of the rock throwers. And neither would He apply it to the woman lost in sin.

"Jesus straightened up and asked her, "Woman, where are they? Has no one condemned you?

"No one, sir," she said. "Then neither do I condemn you," Jesus declared..."[3]

Jesus revealed sovereign love and it looked like mercy. His statement resounded through the city streets, the nation, the world, and 2000 years later it rings powerful and true, "you are forgiven!"

But Jesus wasn't finished!

While He wasn't ever going to throw rocks, neither was He going to leave the woman in her brokenness.

---

[3]*See John 8:7-11,* NIV

The story doesn't end with extravagant mercy. Jesus didn't come just to forgive our sin. He also came to empower us into righteousness. He came to set us free, and not just from a sinful past, but truly and fully free to live a righteous future.

The next thing Jesus said to the woman is just as beautiful, just as life changing, just as extravagant as what's already been proclaimed.

"Go and sin no more."[3]

Understand, this was no fairytale romance; nor was this the typical Hollywood version of an affair, this woman was lost in the great desperation of sin. The fella she was sleeping with wasn't standing next to her in some romantic gesture. While he may have slinked off when they were first discovered, it's just as likely he was one of those holding a rock.

My point, this woman wasn't finding her identity or some great freedom in an affair; she was simply trying to survive in the devastating reality of a control narrative.

And Jesus wasn't going to leave her imprisoned to that great insecurity. He came to "*seek and to save the lost.*"[4] He came to set us free and to make us sure in the sovereignty of His love.

Sovereign Love forgave her when He said, "*Neither will I accuse you.*"

And sovereign Love empowered her when He said, "*Go and sin no more.*"

Jesus wasn't suggesting this woman would never sin, He was releasing grace so she could live as a saint. He was revealing sovereign love – the power of the gospel unto salvation.

Jesus never released mercy without following with grace. Empowerment always follows forgiveness. Sovereign Love forgave and then gave her access to her true identify. She didn't have to live lost in sin. She could live found in Christ.

---

[3]*John 8:7-11,* NIV
[4]*See Luke 19:10,* NIV

She could be free from the bondage of adultery. Free from the prison of feeling value through giving herself sexually to another. Free from the lie that she got her identity from her behavior.

By the way, that's always the lie the theology of sovereign control propagates.

Behavior or Identity

A lot of Christians get saved and, because of poor teaching, take the old paradigm, the old mindset they had before they were saved, into their Christian walk.

Before salvation, everything in life was determined by sin and behavior. But after salvation, we are invited to discover our new identity in Christ. Jesus purchased for us access to sonship. We are sons and daughters of our good and loving Father.

Salvation is the doorway from control to love, from behavior to identity.

But if we, as believers, superimpose a control seeking God into our new narrative, we unintentionally determine that our sin is greater than His love. Then behavior becomes the compass by which we navigate our relationships, both with God and each other.

But the truth is, when we said *yes* to God, we moved from the unforgiving performance based reality of control, to the merciful grace empowering reality of love.

I write about this in depth in my book *Prone to Love,* but in short, our identity has nothing to do with our behavior and everything to do with His mercy and grace. Our identity has been redeemed, in Christ, we are no longer sinners, we are saints!

It's not that behavior isn't important, it's that behavior follows identity. I am not undermining the need for living righteous; I am shifting mindsets regarding the nature of our relationship with God.

Jesus revealed and gave us access to our good Father so we could become sure in our identity as sons and daughters. He gave us the whole story of sovereign love so we could know the Truth that empowers us to live free.

Freedom and Transformation

Much of the church today is better known for what it's against. Why? Because much of the church believes God is sovereignly in control. This belief has forced us to pick up rocks and throw them at the stranger lost and broken in sin until one day that stranger is our friend or family member and we just can't throw rocks anymore.

But because we are trapped by a theology of control, we trade one bondage for another.

Now we are forced to pretend the sin isn't killing the sinner; forced to justify and even defend the broken persons right to be broken. In the name of Jesus, we water down truth and love so it has no power to set free and transform.

So many Christians, trapped in the control narrative, throw rocks and call them truth. They scream principles at the lost, frothing at the mouth, "Be free!"

Truth isn't a principle; Truth is a Person. He sets people free. And He never throws rocks, *"Neither will I accuse you."*

And so many Christians, trapped in the control narrative, are lost in the moral abyss of empathy. They have rightly decided not to throw rocks but that's left them with no other option but to endorse depravity, to actually celebrate brokenness and call it love.

Love isn't empathy; Love is a Person. He always forgives and empowers transformation - *"Neither will I accuse you...go and sin no more."*

Sovereign Love redeems and restores. Sovereign Love reveals our Father's authority and power, sets us free from a life enslaved to behavior modification and gives us access to our identity as righteous sons and daughters.

A Sixth Rule for Being Interviewed

It's been many years since that first interview. I have grown surer in love and, along the way, I've added to the "rules of being interviewed."

There is one final rule I want to highlight in this chapter. For the sake of symmetry, let's title it my sixth rule for being interviewed – *I don't owe the world an answer, I owe them an encounter...*

"What do you think that scripture means?" he asked with just a hint of antagonism.

"That's a good question." I responded. "What does it mean to you?"

My interviewer suddenly seemed uncomfortable, maybe even a little irritated. I think he felt it was his role to ask questions and it was my role to answer them. It's a fair determination, except for one problem, his question was a trap.

He had smugly attempted to position me with one of two options - throw rocks or water down truth. Those weren't options I felt obliged to entertain.

There was an awkward pause. I smiled generously and waited, quite possibly enjoying the irony. He was trapped by his own question.

He made a couple shaky attempts at an answer. I could see the panic begin to show in his eyes. I remembered rule number five, *I'm not here for me, I'm here to love him.* I extended an olive branch - mercy...and then of course, grace. I rephrased his question in such a way that I could introduce *The Answer.*

Here's the deal, I don't owe the world answers; I owe the world an encounter with *The Answer.* I will not throw rocks. Neither will I engage in empathetic reasoning. I will live as a revelation of sovereign love.

The Answer is the whole story; it's not just our perspective, it's His. *The Answer* has power and authority. *The Answer* releases mercy and grace, it sets free, empowers transformation and gives us access to our identity in Christ.

The Answer is the *light that dispels the darkness*; it's the way of seeing that pulls heavens reality to earth. *The Answer* is the resurrection life Jesus revealed and promised us.

I am passionate about revealing sovereign love because I'm convinced a greater revelation will change the world.

And this is not my mandate alone. We, as believers, have all been given mercy and grace to live sure in love and powerfully free as sons and daughters. And we all owe the world an encounter with this love.

chapter ten

I DON'T KNOW... BUT GOD IS GOOD

Karen Knows

"What kind of cloud is that dad?" My seven-year-old, Eva, asked.

"I don't know," I said, then I confidently I followed with, "They are wispy clouds!"

"They're beautiful!" Eva said.

"Yes, they, are!"

We drove the country road in silence enjoying the beautiful wispy clouds. But, out of my peripheral, I could see what was coming and I smiled.

After about a minute Karen spoke up, "They are Cirrus clouds Eva."

I shook my head in mock disappointment, "There you go again, complicating beautiful things with information. They look like wispy clouds to me, Eva."

Karen smiled, "Yes Eva, but they are called Cirrus clouds." She held up her phone to show us both that God, I mean, Google, had spoken. Then she looked at me and stuck out her tongue.

And I remember a simpler time, before Google; a time when it was OK to say, *"I don't know,"* a time before one needed to know the Latin term to enjoy wispy clouds…

I Don't Know

Shortly after my book *Prone to Love* released I came across a review. The reviewer was an earnest believer who graciously but systematically challenged many of my conclusions regarding the sovereignty of God's always-good love.

The review was thorough, the disagreement thoughtful, surgical and, because of the reviewer's sincerity and the use of scripture to support each challenge, convincing.

As I read it, I felt anxious. Not because I was unsure regarding what I had written. I was sure. And not because the reviewer disagreed, I don't need agreement. It was how the reviewer used scripture to methodically undermine the truths I had written. I felt a heavy obligation to systematically respond to each question raised. There was one problem, I wasn't confident I could provide convincing systematic answers.

The next time I sat down to write, instead of further developing the book I was working on, a book about sovereign love, this book, I began to develop a rebuttal.

I opened a new Word Doc on my MacBook. But after only ten minutes of writing, I began to feel frustrated. If I responded to each scripture reference, I would be at it for days, maybe even weeks; and after all that, I wasn't sure I would be able to deliver convincing answers.

Then, I sensed God laughing good-naturedly. I stopped writing and quieted my heart.

"What are you doing?" He asked.

"I'm trying to get answers to the scriptures used in that review." I responded.

"How's it going?" He asked.

"Not great; it's a little overwhelming." I responded.

"Well, whatever you do, don't make them up."

That made me smile. "Father, You are so good. I love You."

"I love you." He replied, settling my heart.

I slid my little MacBook navigation arrow up to the left corner of my new Word Doc. I clicked the dark grey dot, which triggered the on-screen prompt, *"Do you want to save the changes you made to this document?"*

"Don't Save," I clicked, smiling again, all anxiety gone. Then I went back to writing where I felt grace; I leaned into His pleasure.

My Father's kind interruption had done two things. First, He identified the source of my anxiety. I had started defending instead of revealing.

Many years earlier I had come to the freeing realization that God doesn't desire, nor need to be defended, but He loves to be revealed.

And I love to reveal Him. It's my great joy to seek after and reveal His perfect love nature, to discover wisdom that I might have answers to the questions. That's why I love Proverbs 4:7.

"The beginning of wisdom is this: Get wisdom. Though it cost all you have, get understanding."

Wisdom, it's both a gift and mandate and we have been both invited and instructed to seek after it until we have understanding. And this world needs men and women who have wisdom and understanding – who have the answers. Answers to the questions around relationships, politics, economics, science… This world needs leaders confident in the sovereignty of love.

As believers, it's not just our joy to discover the answers; it's our honor to reveal them. And as Christians, we have all felt the cultural pressure, the expectation to provide the answers – all of them, even when we don't yet know.

That's why I believe this next phrase is one every Christian should learn; it's a phrase that is most important to our spiritual growth.

I don't know...

Living in the Tension

Now back to the contrary review of my last book.

As I mentioned, my Father's gracious interruption of my brief attempt to write a rebuttal had done two things. The second? He empowered me to live in the tension of not knowing. He removed from me the anxious striving to have all the answers and in so doing, He invited me into the process of wisdom and understanding.

I don't know... is the humble gift we offer to the One who wants nothing more than to reveal Himself more fully to us. *I don't know* frees and then empowers us to discover – to experience revelation.

Revelation is simply seeing what was always there. It's a veil removed so we can know. All humanity is designed for a greater revelation of God's love.

But you can't fill a glass that's already full. My point, greater revelation is only available to those who walk with the humble awareness that they don't have it all figured out yet.

We must value mystery as much as we value revelation; we must be willing to position ourselves in a question if we want to experience and know the answers.

The willingness to live by faith in the tension of an unanswered question is what positions us for *the* answer that transforms. A humble and hungry "I don't know" will lead us into wisdom and understanding.

I don't know is the invitation to discover His goodness in greater measure. Because, while there is plenty I don't know, there is one thing I am absolutely positive about; God is good. It's my position on everything.

I don't know, but God is good. That phrase has been one of our family and ministry mottos for years. It's a faith statement that has served us well.

The first half of that statement is extremely powerful only because we believe the second half with absolute conviction. We have made it our position on everything.

Why did we experience a miscarriage? *I don't know, but God is good.*

Why did we lose our business? *I don't know, but God is good.*

Why are we not experiencing breakthrough in ministry, in family, in healing, in the promises of God? *I don't know, but God is good.*

Why are we being persecuted for loving the lost, choosing honor, seeking His presence, revealing family, hoping where there is no hope, giving beyond comfortable, choosing life, living wildly faithful...

I don't know, but God is good is the position of faith that empowers us to live between the tension of not knowing and His invitation to know, *to get wisdom and understanding.*

Doubting Thomas?

Years ago, I overheard my mom in the kitchen telling my sister, Aimee, how Thomas was her favorite disciple of Jesus.

I was a little surprised by her choice and thought I'd be clever.

"Mom, I don't want to be a doubting Thomas, but I'm pretty sure your favorite disciple was the fella with the underwhelming moniker." I yelled into the kitchen sarcastically.

My mom came out of the kitchen and gave me a fiery look. One I saw too many times in my youth; a look that releases the awe-inspiring fear of God, "Jason, it's just horrible we call him that! Think about the scripture we have because Thomas was bold enough to ask when the others weren't?"

And just like that, my whole thought about Thomas changed. Thanks, mom! I am so grateful for your wisdom!

Jesus, attempting to prepare His disciples for the coming dark days of His death, tells them, *"You know the way to the place where I am going."*[1]

And John leans over to Peter and whispers. "Hey Pete?"

"What?" Peter responds in a whisper yell. Peter was a horrible whisperer.

"Do you know the way to the place Jesus is going?" John asks with sincerity.

Peter furrows his brow, "Of course!"

John raises an eyebrow, "So you have no idea then."

Peter waves John off brusquely. John is a little concerned but then he remembers and smiles, "No worries, Thomas will ask Him."

And Thomas did. And we are all infinitely glad he did.

"Thomas said to him, "Lord, we don't know where you are going, so how can we know the way?"[2]

"We don't know..." It was nice Thomas included the other disciples, but because of his question we all have an answer, and it's one of our all-time favorites!

"Jesus answered, 'I am the way and the truth and the life. No one comes to the Father except through me. If you really know me, you will know my Father as well. From now on, you do know him and have seen him.'"[2]

Thomas' *"we don't know"* makes room for Jesus to highlight the tension of mystery and revelation, *"You will know"* and *"From now on, you do know..."* Jesus' answer is the beautiful invitation to live in the tension of not knowing with a promise of knowing.

---

[1]*John 14:4,* NIV
[2]*John 14:5-7,* NIV

Like always, Jesus is speaking in the infinite language of sovereign love…

John and Peter looked at each other after Jesus was finished. They still didn't understand, but that wasn't unusual. Jesus was always saying stuff that was not only confusing, but also often seriously controversial.

The fact is, most of the time, most of the people listening to Jesus had little to no idea what He was talking about.

One time Jesus told His followers that the only way they could experience eternal life was if they ate His flesh and drank His blood. A lot of people stopped following Jesus that day. When Jesus asked the twelve disciples if they would leave Him also, Peter famously said, *"Lord, to whom shall we go, you have the words of eternal life."*[3]

Interpretation, *"I don't know… but God is good"* and that's enough.

Peter, John, Thomas and many others have revealed that to truly follow Jesus, we must be willing to live in the tension of not knowing and the invitation to know; to *"get wisdom. Though it cost all (we) have, get understanding."*

We must embrace mystery if we are to gain revelation.

Jesus is *the way* to where we are going; He is the lens by which to discover *wisdom,* the key by which to unlock *understanding.*

I don't call Thomas "doubting" anymore. He was a man of faith willing to live in the tension of the question so he might discover the whole story, the greater revelation. Thomas gave everything up to follow Jesus and after He ascended to heaven, Thomas is believed to have shared the gospel of sovereign love, planting churches in Syria, Babylon (Iraq), Persia (Iran) and even into India before dying by a spear, martyred for his profound faith in *the way the truth and the life.*

Karen Knows

I love Karen. She is a knower; she not only enjoys knowing, she *has*

---

[3]*John 6:68,* NIV

to know. Karen has to know what the movie is about before we watch it, how many hours the flight is before we get on the airplane, and what the ingredients are in everything we eat. Mostly, I love that she knows, but sometimes I just want to know by watching the movie, getting there when we get there and eating it because it tastes good.

But nearly 25 years with Karen has taught me that there is great wisdom in knowing.

Knowing,

- what to do in the event of a grease fire
- what a baby copperhead looks like
- the expiration date on the pork
- how to do our taxes
- about the evils of processed foods

Karen is the steady force in my life, the reason our family functions with peace and grace. We're a good team, she makes sure I know what day it is, I make sure there's organic fair trade coffee in the morning.

But when it comes to a life of faith, sometimes knowing isn't an option. Sometimes, and Karen would tell you this as well, being willing to lean into the mystery of not know is the only way to discover the joy of greater revelation.

Nicodemus

"Master, we know that you are a teacher from God, for no one performs the miracle signs that you do, unless God's power is with him."[4]

Jesus responded to Nicodemus, a member of the Jewish ruling council, a well-educated leader, a socially elite Pharisee who had snuck out late one night for a covert meeting with Him, *"Nicodemus, listen to this eternal truth: You can perceive the kingdom realm of God, but you must first experience a rebirth."*[4]

---

[4]*John 3:1-15 The Passion Translation TPT*

Nicodemus didn't know what Jesus was talking about. *"Rebirth? How can a grey-headed man be reborn? It's impossible for a man to go back into the womb a second time and be reborn!"*[4]

Then Jesus began to describe the whole story through the mystery of salvation, *"I speak an eternal truth: Unless you are born of water and Spirit-wind, you will never enter the kingdom realm of God. For the natural realm can only give birth to things that are natural, but the spiritual realm gives birth to supernatural life!"*[4]

Jesus revealed how we enter this new narrative, the whole story, we must experience a rebirth.

Then Jesus speaks plainly to Nicodemus using the example of wind, something Nicodemus understood, to introduce a mystery. *"You shouldn't be amazed by my statement, 'You must be born from above!' For the spirit-wind blows as it chooses. You can hear its sound, but you don't know where it came from or where it's going. So it is within the hearts of those who are Spirit-born!"*[4]

Essentially Jesus is saying, "You can't see the wind. You know not from where it originates and where it goes, but its evidence can't be denied. To experience the wind is to embrace its mystery. You must be born again..."

And Nicodemus would not lean into the mystery, *"How does this happen?"* He asks.

"Aren't you the respected teacher in Israel, and yet you don't understand this revelation?[4] Essentially Jesus is saying, "How can you teach people about the hidden mysteries of my nature if you can't even accept what is in front of your eyes?"

"I speak eternal truths about things I know, things I have seen and experienced-and still you don't accept what I reveal.[4] "I am doing miracles; you've seen them, you don't have to understand them to know they tell a greater story, they reveal a truer narrative."

"If you're unable to understand and believe what I have told you about

---

[4]*John 3:1-15 The Passion Translation TPT*

the natural realm, what will you do when I begin to unveil the heavenly realm?"[4]

Jesus is saying, "I have just spoken plainly, in the language of earth, where two plus two always equals four, but you don't understand? Heaven isn't simple math. Sovereign love is measureless. It's transcends time and space; its greater than the beginning and the end. It's beyond your ability to know. It surpasses intellect. It requires that you be willing to live in the mystery of not knowing while seeking revelation.

If you don't have enough faith to perceive me through earthly concepts such as birth and wind, how will you perceive the measureless revelation of sovereign love?"

Paul describes this measureless love in Ephesians when he prayed that we would "*... know this love that surpasses knowledge—that (we) may be filled to the measure of all the fullness of God...*"[5]

Jesus is essentially saying, "How are you going *to know a love that surpasses knowledge,* how are you going *to be filled to measure of all the fullness* of an immeasurable God, if you are unwilling to embrace the unknown even when you can see the evidence?"

I would like to suggest that a lot of the theology in our churches, and therefore our planet, is birthed from believers who were unwilling to embrace the tension of *I don't know* and *get wisdom.* Instead of living by faith in the mystery of sovereign love, much of the church has answered the unknown with sovereign control.

We have settled in the natural realm when Jesus revealed and invited us to live from the heavenly realm. We have decided we would rather have *a theology of control* than live in the tension of not knowing.

The fact is, we live in a culture that demands answers. And we owe them the answers. But to truly know, to truly grow in understanding, to truly discover the answer, is to embrace the mystery of sovereign love.

---

[4]*John 3:1-15 The Passion Translation TPT*
[5]*See Ephesians 3:19*

Not Knowing

In a theology of sovereign control, a sense of security is always found in knowing. The mystery of not knowing isn't really an option - there must be absolute answers.

But in a theology of sovereign love, not knowing is a beautiful opportunity for greater revelation. Not knowing is the authentic invitation to discover how our Father thinks and sees. In the freedom of sovereign love, we can live in the tension of mystery and grow ever sure in His goodness.

In many ways, science and human intellect have become the measuring stick by which to determine the nature of God. But the discovery of God is not possible solely through intellectual pursuit.

I am not dismissing the mind, but we are to love the Lord our God with all our *heart, soul, strength and mind.*[6] There is a reason Jesus ordered it that way. The heart speaks the language of heaven because the heart is where mystery can be engaged through faith.

What the heart believes the mind perceives.

The fact is, the sovereignty of God can't be fully understood, it can only be experienced. This book isn't an attempt to answer all the questions on the sovereignty of God; it's an invitation to lean into the mystery, to get wisdom, and to grow in the revelation of His always good love.

"The beginning of wisdom is this: Get wisdom. Though it cost all you have, get understanding."

Wisdom is the gift given to those willing to embrace mystery in the search for greater revelation.

Understanding is discovered by those willing to live in the tension of not knowing while never leaving the conviction that He is good.

---

[6]*See Luke 10:27*

The answers are imparted to those who have made intimacy the answer…

I recently stumbled across that contrary review – the one that had briefly caused such anxiety years ago. You know what's funny? I can answer the questions raised in that article now. In fact, I was surprised to realize I had unknowingly answered many of them in this book.

I wasn't looking for *an* answer, I wanted revelation.

And I have learned that revelation is always discovered in the faith of "*I don't know, but God is good.*"

chapter eleven

PUT YOUR SWORD AWAY!

Put Your Sword Away!

"I don't understand," races through Peters mind over and again.

Shaking and disoriented, he breaths heavy. There's blood everywhere, it's spattered across Jesus robe. Peter can taste the iron saltiness of it on his lips. He stands frantic with desperation over a mutilated piece of flesh. Angry tears blur his vision; he grits his teeth and, with trembling hands, moves to strike again.

"Put your sword away!" Jesus commands.[1]

Peter barely recognizes his Lord and friends voice. The night is full with panic and horror. Jesus speaks again, His words weighted and resolute.

"Shall I not drink the cup the Father has given me?"[2]

---

[1] *Matthew 26:52,* NLT
[2] *John 18:10-11,* NLT

It felt like a fist to the gut; everything Peter believed, being sifted like wheat.

Peter watches as Jesus leans over the man he just struck with his sword. The man, now on his knees, whimpers as he clutches violently at the right side of his head; blood running between his fingers, down his arm, dripping from his elbow.

Jesus leaned over him *"touched the man's ear and healed him."*[3]

And Peter has seen this so many times, Jesus kindness, His goodness, His healing, His sovereign love.

"I don't understand" races through his mind again as Jesus, the man he loved, the man he followed with all his strength, the man he had just given his life for, admonishes him, *"All who draw the sword will die by the sword..."*[4]

"I don't understand," tormented Peter as he followed the prisoner Jesus through dark city streets and finally into the temple grounds.

"I don't understand," ravaged his heart as he denied he knew the man he loved, once, twice, three times.

"I don't understand," wrecked his soul as he caught Jesus' eye from across the courtyard just as the rooster crowed.

"I don't understand" sifted all of him like wheat as he fled the temple grounds.

"And he went out and wept bitterly."[5]

Just hours earlier, Peter thought he understood; he thought he knew. He promised he'd never deny Jesus, *"Lord I'm ready to go with you to prison or death."*[6]

Just hours earlier, Peter believed Jesus kingdom on earth would need swords and men willing to use them. It would require sacrifice, the willingness to die for Jesus, and also, the willingness to kill for Jesus.

---

[3] *Luke 22:51,* NLT
[4] *Matthew 26:52,* NIV
[5] *John 22:62,* ESV
[6] *Luke 22:33,* NIV

The theology of control perverts everything, even our passionate love of God! Sovereign control manipulates love into a desperate defense of our broken ideology.

We see it evidenced throughout history, well-meaning Christians committed to murder in order to defend their idea of God.

The mindset is alive today. Open up Facebook and you'll see it, well-meaning Christians attacking others to defend their idea of God.

It's everywhere, well-meaning Christians preaching from church pulpits, political platforms, across the web and airwaves, attacking a person or organization in order to defend their idea of God.

Well-meaning Christians destroying families and friendships and derailing great moves of God; well-meaning Christians manipulating scripture to develop cult like devotion to the desperate defense of ideologies absolutely contrary to the revelation of Jesus.

Understand, Peter didn't truly defend Jesus; he truly defended his belief about Jesus. My point? While Peter's defense was true, it wasn't the truth that sets free.

Peter believed that, if the kingdom was to be established on earth as it is in heaven, at some point Jesus must assume control. There are still so many Christians today who believe this…

Except, Jesus never once modeled this.

Peter's belief in the lie of sovereign control ultimately set him against the very revelation of Jesus and led him to do something perversely contrary to sovereign love.

The control narrative is so perversely deceitful. It led a man who had walked with Jesus for three years to believe killing another person was the only way to advance the kingdom; that murder was the way to bring heaven to earth.

Please get this, if your understanding of God leads to anxiety and fear, you don't truly understand. *Put your sword away!*

If your love of God leads you to act out of fear, you need a greater revelation of His love. *Put your sword away!*

If you feel you *must* attack someone in order to defend your thoughts about God, it's a good sign your thoughts about God are wrong. *Put your sword away!*

If you find yourself desperate and insecure on God's behalf, you don't have the whole story. *Put your sword away!*

Desperation is not a sign of spiritual maturity, it's a sign we are not yet sure in sovereign love; it's a sign we're still journeying into a greater revelation of His goodness, our minds still being renewed.

Ultimate Love

"If the kingdom is to be established on earth and the enemy is to be destroyed, at some point Jesus must ultimately assume control."

That flawed idea is still alive and well in the church today. It has been presented to me often during the last several years in which I have written this book.

I have had many point to Jesus' second coming and the fact that He will crush the enemy under His feet and establish His rule and reign as the proof that He must have ultimate control.

I absolutely believe Jesus is returning. I absolutely believe He will crush the enemy under His feet[7] and establish His Kingdom.

But why would we think God will use control to crush the enemy and establish His Kingdom upon His return when He didn't use control the first time He walked the earth?

The fact is, the enemy is already done for. Not because God is ultimately in control, but because God is ultimate love. It was finished on a cross over 2000 years ago when God, in the flesh, the perfect revelation

[7] *See Romans 16:20*

of the power and authority of sovereign love, laid down His life even unto death.

Jesus defeated the enemy through an act of ultimate love - sacrificial surrender and then resurrection life. In so doing, Jesus powerfully revealed that He doesn't need to be in control to establish His rule and reign, to see His Kingdom victorious.

Please get this, the idea that ultimate control is the only way to win is actually how Satan thinks.

The enemy's approach in the Garden of Gethsemane was control through force and he lost. Jesus' approach in the garden was perfect love through sacrificial surrender and He won. I would like to suggest that has always been, and will always be God's approach.

The extent to which we believe God must have ultimate control, either now or in the future, is the extent to which we will find ourselves operating like Peter in the garden. Desperate, insecure and ultimately counter to the gospel of ultimate love.

Have You Ever Met This Jesus Follower?

I have often thought the story would be more entertaining if Peter had actually succeeded in his attempt to remove the servant's head with his sword. I like to imagine what that miracle would have been like. Alas, Peter was a fisherman. He was useless with a sword!

I've also often wondered how the servant would have felt after his traumatic de-earing and then miraculous re-earing.

"Hey buddy, how are you doing? How's the ear? The pain is gone? Wow!

Hey, quick question. How do you feel about Jesus?

Yes, He IS awesome! Here you are, about to arrest Him, about to reign down brutal violence upon Him, and He heals you? Amazing!

Yes, I agree, His kindness will change your life forever.

Hey, one more question. How do you feel about Jesus' followers…"

Have you ever been in a relationship with a desperate follower of Jesus? I have. There's a lot of ducking involved…

Peter represented the Kingdom of control and it looked like desperation and pain and force and led to death. Then Jesus represented the Kingdom of Love and it looked like grace and healing and surrender and led to resurrection life.

Which Kingdom representation do you think truly leads to a transformed life?

If you have ever tasted even a hint of the love of God, the answer is obvious.

What would happen if the church represented the King and His Kingdom like Jesus did in the garden instead of like Peter?

I Don't Know the Man

I'm not taking away from the weight of his verbal denial of Jesus, but I would like to propose that Peter's first denial didn't take place in the temple grounds just before the rooster crowed. No, Peters first denial took place the moment he attempted murder on Jesus' behalf. It took place when he tried to kill another person in order to protect his understanding.

"I don't know the man," That's what Peter said later in the temple grounds. And to some extent, it was true. Peter was simply verbalizing his most recent experience. He thought he understood, thought he knew, but he didn't have the whole story and because of it, he got it very wrong.

When Jesus confronted Peters murderous action and then healed the de-eared servant, the lie Peter believed about the nature of God was suddenly exposed. Peter was devastated. The very foundation, his theology of control, was wrong. Somehow, he had missed it. And that was when *all of* Peter *was sifted like wheat.*

To Sift All of You as Wheat

"Simon, Simon (Peter), Satan has asked to sift all of you as wheat. But I have prayed for you, Simon, that your faith may not fail. And when you have turned back, strengthen your brothers."[8]

Satan has no power but deception. He is not all knowing, all seeing, all hearing; he is a limited being created by God. Jesus has *all authority*, He has given us this authority, Satan therefore, has no authority but what we give him. Therefore, Satan can't do anything without our permission.

I would like to propose the lie of control was so powerfully a part of Peter's understanding that Satan had access and influence regarding Peter's emotions and actions. So, when Satan asked to sift Peter like wheat, he was simply acknowledging the fact that Peter had already given him permission. That's right, Peter.

Jesus didn't say, "I gave Satan permission," He said, ""*But I have prayed for you, Simon (Peter), that your faith may not fail. And when you have turned back, strengthen your brothers."*

Essentially, "Peter, you are so deceived by a theology of control that you can't *truly* see me. This will ultimately position you with the enemy and lead you to deny me. *But I have prayed for your faith* so you may see me for who I *truly* am, sovereign love; so you may repent, so your mind can be renewed, so you can be set free and empowered to strengthen your brothers."

If we believe God is in sovereign control, we will actually use this interaction between Satan and God in scripture to prove that a God in control allowed Satan to sift Peter as wheat. As if Jesus somehow partnered with Satan to grow Peter's faith.

It's a ridiculous and devastating perspective.

God never partners with Satan to grow our faith. That thought comes directly from the pit of hell. It's the fruit of the control narrative and it is passed time we stopped believing it!

---

[8] *Luke 22:31-32*, NIV

The enemy is always seeking to sift us as wheat and what we believe about God determines his access and influence.

But there is good news - Jesus is praying for our faith!

Transition

When we take the journey of faith, we leave one paradigm to discover another; we leave the broken theology of control that revolves around fear and manipulation to enter the revelation of sovereign love.

Faith leads to the discovery of an upside-down kingdom; a kingdom in which the last are first,[9] the least are the greatest,[10] the weak are strong,[11] the poor are rich,[12] and we lay our life down to find it.[13]

In the garden, Peter was transitioning from one theology to another and it would require great faith in the power and authority of sovereign love.

Faith invites us to live in the tension of not knowing and yet still believe He is good. This faith exposes the lie and shifts our theology until we see from heaven's perspective and are set free.

It's why faith is so essential, why God Himself was praying for it, and why He is so pleased when we walk it out.[14]

Faith

After the resurrection, Jesus met Peter on a beach and three times restored him with the question, "*Do you love me?*"

"He (Peter) said, "Lord, you know all things; you know that I love you."[15]

Peter, after being asked the question for a third time, answered, *"Lord you know."*

"Lord you know." That answer reveals a man God can trust with a

[9]*See Matthew 20:16*
[10]*See Luke 9:48*
[11]*See 2 Corinthians 12:9*
[12]*See James 2:5*
[13]*See Matthew 10:39*
[14]*See Hebrews 11:6*
[15]*John 21:17*, NIV

sword. Not a physical sword, this was no desperate forceful extension of the arm, this was infinitely more powerful than that. This was a greater revelation – the confident authority and power of ultimate sovereign love.

"Peter, do you love me?"

Jesus asked until Peter could say yes. And this *yes* was not birthed from self-dependence, it was birthed from surrender. Just like Jesus, Peter learned that the enemy is defeated and the Kingdom established through sacrificial love.

This *yes* would not lead to the desperation he experienced in the garden, this wasn't about living in fear of death. This *yes* was empowered by the transformative grace of resurrection life. This *yes* would not further the control narrative, it would establish sovereign love on earth as it is in heaven.

I would like to suggest that the interaction on the beach wasn't about whether Peter loved Jesus; that was never really in question. Peter loved Jesus enough to die for him. He had already proved it. But loving God is not what sets us free; it's not what transforms us. Loving God isn't even what saves us.

Loving God is a response, and this is only possible to the extent we have revelation regarding the perfection of His sovereign love for us. Our revelation of God's sovereign love for us is what sets free, transforms and saves.

"We love because He first loved."[16]

This whole story, from the garden to the beach, was about where Peter would put His faith. Would it be in his understanding, in his wisdom or knowledge, in his passion, in his love for God? Or would it be in God's always-good love for him?

Here is another way to describe it. Peter lived with a theology of

---

[16] *1 John 4:19*, NIV

sovereign control. His faith was therefore based in his behavior. Its ultimate conclusion was desperation and death, both the willingness to die and the willingness to kill. The sovereign control narrative always leads to death.

Jesus defined it this way, *"those who live by the sword die by the sword."* That may be the best description of sovereign control on the planet.

Jesus was leading Peter into freedom, he was inviting him to no longer place his faith in sovereign control but instead in sovereign love.

Sovereign love also invites us to die, but not in desperation and never in partnership with death. No, the invitation to *take up our cross and follow Him* is always the invitation to resurrection life. It's the invitation to live in freedom and grace, confident that sovereign love always redeems, renews and restores.

Jesus died, and rose so death would not be our narrative.

The good news is that, in the narrative of sovereign love, we *get* to die!

We get to die to the bondage of sin, the bondage of fear and anxiety and shame, and every other fruit of control. And then we get to live again! Transformed, sure in the perfection of love, confident in the power and authority of sovereign love. And free, so wonderfully free!

In the garden, Peter attempted murder because of his zealous love for Jesus. It nearly killed him. *Those who live by the sword...* Our faith can never be in our love of God.

In the garden, Peter attempted murder in defense of what he knew. It nearly destroyed him. *Those who live by the sword...* Our faith can never be in what we know.

In the garden, Peter attempted murder to help Jesus assume control. It led to bitter sorrow. *Those who live by the sword...* Our faith can never be in sovereign control.

Our faith must be in the sovereignty of His love.

And when it is, we can be trusted with a sword.

And how does Jesus reveal the sword?

Then Jesus said, *"Feed my sheep..."*

Feed My Sheep

We are all in transition from one narrative to another. Following God will often lead us into gardens where we will come face to face with our broken paradigms, our flawed premises will be exposed, we will experience sifting. But, if by faith we contend for His always good love, this sifting will leave us humbled and clear eyed. It will redeem our perspective.

"But even if you should suffer for what is right, you are blessed. Do not fear their threats; do not be frightened. But in your hearts revere Christ as Lord..."[17]

These words can be found in 1st Peter 3:14. These words came from the same Peter who attempted murder to protect His ideology. Where was the transformation? On a beach where Peters eyes could truly see the wonder and power and great freedom of sovereign love.

To this day, Peters revelation is still feeding sheep. You and I are the evidence of Peter's faith in sovereign love.

The revelation of sovereign love will set us free so we never have to live desperate or afraid. It will empower us to love God authentically, without reserve, it will lead to great intimacy, it will increase the depth of our passion for His love nature.

And it will transform us into love, and empower us to love others truly and powerfully generous.

Jesus redeemed the narrative, He gave us access to the whole story. And when we live from freedom, not for it, we too can feed His sheep.

---

[17] *1 Peter 3:14,* NIV

chapter twelve

TESTING

His Name was Will Hunting

The first time I met the kid I liked him. He was arrogant, condescending and very lost; he reminded me of myself at his age.

I had been told he was a genius, a bona fide math prodigy. But what I saw was an orphan from a Boston South End neighborhood trying to prove he had nothing to prove.

We met in my office. We spared, a test of words. He mocked the books on my shelf as "the wrong books." It was a boast of superior intellect. He ridiculed a painting I had painted with a condescending grasp of art history. And to be honest, he struck me to the heart with his ignorant and ruthless comments about my wife. He assumed, with great arrogance, that he knew me.

Even as I informed him our time was up, I knew I could help him.

I set up a second session…

Child Sacrifice

There is nothing more perverse or heart wrenchingly evil than an intentional act to harm a child. There are truly no words to capture such brokenness.

"Then God said, "Take your son, your only son, whom you love—Isaac—and go to the region of Moriah. Sacrifice him there as a burnt offering on a mountain I will show you."[1]

Child sacrifice is the vilest act in the existence of humanity, the utmost perversion of worship imaginable.

For the sake of my heart, I did the minimal amount of research necessary to write this piece. It wrecked me. The sheer viciousness; babies and children brutally killed as acts of demented worship to appease the controlling deity of their day. You see, child sacrifice has existed in some form in nearly every culture since the fall.

It still exists today. It's victims in the millions in America alone. Babies sacrificed to the controlling god of humanism, mothers and fathers crushed under the weight of such devastating worship, all enslaved to a paradigm of fear, condemnation and shame...

"Early the next morning Abraham got up and loaded his donkey. He took with him two of his servants and his son Isaac. When he had cut enough wood for the burnt offering, he set out for the place God had told him about."[2]

Burning your child on an alter is how it was done in Abraham's day. In the narrative Abraham was familiar with, in the land of Canaan where he lived, the sacrifice of the firstborn was customary. In times of trouble, the Canaanites offered their best and dearest to the gods, *"the fruit of their body for the sin of their soul."*[3]

And that's the perfect description of what a worship sacrifice looks like in the control narrative; propitiation birthed from desperation; fear driven butchery performed to curry favor with one more powerful lest he destroy you.

---

[1]*Genesis 22:1,* NIV
[2]*Genesis 22:2,* NIV
[3]*See Micah 6:7*

Child sacrifice is the most desperate act of a slave struggling to ease the harsh reality of his or her existence. The sacrifice of innocence is the ultimate horrific demand of the sovereign control narrative.

His Name was Will Hunting

"What's this, a taster's choice moment between guys?"[4]

That's how he started in our second session. Then he made a crass remark about the geese that were swimming in the pond just across from where we were sitting. I'd moved our meeting to the park. We sat on a bench overlooking the water.

It was a perfect Boston Fall day.

I didn't acknowledge his sarcasm. I knew about his past. He was lost and angry. I went at him straight on.

"I thought about what you said to me the other day. About my wife... Stayed up half the night thinking about it. Then something occurred to me and I fell into a deep peaceful sleep and I haven't thought about you since. You know what occurred to me?"

"No"

"You're just a kid. You haven't the faintest idea what you're talking about. You think you know something because you read it in a book? It requires living it."[4]

And Then...

"To Abraham, not unfamiliar with various ways in which among his heathen ancestors, the deity was propitiated, the testing question comes, 'Is he prepared to obey his God as fully as the people around him obey their god?"

- Translated from, The Early Religion of Israel, by Robertson.

"Early the next morning Abraham got up and loaded his donkey. He

---

[4]*Quotes from the movie, "Good Will Hunting"*

took with him two of his servants and his son Isaac. When he had cut enough wood for the burnt offering, he set out for the place God had told him about."[5]

I don't know about you, but I have never once woken up wondering if today is the day God will require me to murder my child in order to prove my faith. But because of the narrative Abraham lived in, I imagine the reality of child sacrifice was one of his greatest daily fears.

Imagine living in a culture where killing your firstborn is the most powerful way to prove one's devotion. That was the context for Abraham's daily life, the narrative in which he exercised his faith. For Abraham, child sacrifice was less a matter of "if" and more a matter of "when."

Because of the culture and time in which he lived, Abraham actually believed the day might come when God would require that ultimate sacrifice; proof that he would surrender to God's absolute control.

"What if today is the day?"

I imagine that thought plagued his mornings, stalked his days and haunted his nights.

And then, just as he expected, the day arrived.

And he was ready. He didn't debate it, didn't wait to see if he had heard right, didn't 'put out a 'fleece.'[6] He had been preparing for this test. Immediately he set out to offer gruesome devotion in the form of slaughtering his child, his greatest fear becoming his reality.

Abraham, a pioneer in the discovery of the nature of God, a forerunner in the revelation of His goodness, a man growing sure, the father of our faith, packed up his donkey and prepared to commit the greatest perversion of worship ever known, the sickening act of child sacrifice.

"On the third day Abraham looked up and saw the place in the distance. He said to his servants, "Stay here with the donkey while I and the boy go over there. We will worship and..."[7]

[5]*Genesis 22:3*, NIV

[6]*Putting out a fleece was one of the ways Gideon tested whether he had heard God correctly. You can find the story in Judges 6.*

[7]*Genesis 22:5*, NIV

The fact that Abraham described child sacrifice as an act of worship reveals that he lived in bondage to the theology of sovereign control – a paradigm that requires horrific acts of desperation to appease a controlling God.

But the sentence wasn't concluded. Abraham, a pioneer in the discovery of the nature of God, a forerunner in the revelation of His goodness, a man growing sure, the father of our faith, wasn't finished.

There was a powerful conjunction - "*an instance of two or more events or things occurring at the same point in time or space.*"[8]

The conjunction was, "*And then...*"

Abraham said, "*We will worship*

and then

we will come back to you."

This may be the most amazing sentence in Abraham's entire life story.

It tells us two things. The first half of the sentence, "*we will worship,*" reveals that Abraham was so enslaved to the context of his day that he wasn't able to access the truth that would set him free - that God would never require child sacrifice as a form of worship.

The second half of the sentence, "*and then we will both come back,*" reveals that Abraham was a man of powerful faith; he believed with great conviction that God was good. It had been settled. He didn't understand how God would reveal His goodness, He couldn't explain it, but, and here's where it's gets truly amazing, although it had never yet happened, Abraham actually believed God was so good that He would resurrect Isaac. Abraham believed in resurrection life.

"*By faith Abraham, when God tested him, offered Isaac as a sacrifice... Abraham reasoned that God could even raise the dead...*"[9]

And in that place of, "*I don't know,*" Abraham determined, "*but*

---

[8]*Dictionary.com*
[9]*Hebrews 11:17-19,* NIV

God is good." He put his faith in the goodness of God and it's why he is considered to be the "*father of our faith.*"[10]

The fact is, you don't know what you don't know, but faith believes God is always good and that's always more than enough.

His Name was Will Hunting

I had his attention, now it was time to drive the point home. While sitting on that park bench I said,

"When I look at you I don't see an intelligent confident man, I see a cocky, scared kid.

You're an orphan kid from the streets of Boston, right? What if I determined I knew you because I read Oliver Twist? You think you know something because you read it in a book? It requires living it. You don't know what you don't know."

He was quiet. So, I concluded.

"You're move chief."[4]

Who was Truly Tested?

I believe much of the church has interpreted this story of Abraham and Isaac through the lens of sovereign control and because of it, much of the church has lived with a cocky scared theology.

Sovereign control will greatly distort our understanding of testing. I am only describing something I have personally experienced.

You see, I used to think testing was all about me proving my love and devotion for God. But I would like to suggest it's actually the other way around.

When a teacher gives a test, it's fair to say that the teacher is the one who is ultimately being tested. And just in case you were wondering, God is a good teacher.

---

[10]*See Romans 4:16*

[4]*Quotes from the movie, "Good Will Hunting"*

God didn't give Abraham a test so Abraham could prove his love. God gave Abraham a test so God could reveal the goodness of sovereign love in an area where Abraham was devastatingly deceived. God gave Abraham a test so Abraham could perceive the truth and be set free.

I would like to suggest that every test is an invitation into a greater revelation of the truth that sets free. And passing a test is always evidenced by transformed thinking, wholeness and greater intimacy.

We don't know what we don't know. And sometimes, the only way to know is to follow God into our greatest fear so we can experience the whole story of His sovereign love – so we can be set free.

His Name was Will Hunting

I had originally been asked to meet with the kid by a former associate. He was a professor at MIT, one of the most prestigious mathematical universities in the world. And he had personal ambitions for the young man.

In my opinion, his motives were skewed. He was less interested in the kids' well-being and more interested in what he could do.

I was just about to have a session with the young man when the professor walked into my office. He was angry because I wouldn't pressure the kid to concede to his agenda.

"I brought you in here because I wanted you to help me with the boy…Don't you dare undermine what I'm trying to do here." He yelled.

I was angry too and roared back. "It's not about you, it's about the kid! It's about the boy! He is a good kid. And I won't see you make him feel like a failure!"[4]

I had ambitions for the young man as well. I wanted to see him set free from his past; free from thinking and living like an orphan for the rest of his life, free from the lie that he was worthless, free from his inability to be vulnerable, free to trust.

---

[4]*Quotes from the movie, "Good Will Hunting"*

Yes, he was a talented young man, he had a gift and with it a future, but I didn't want his future to be enslaved to his past, or to what he could do. I wanted him free and empowered to a future where he could access trust and know love and intimacy.

The kid was at a crossroads, he was being tested, and I wanted to be a good teacher.

The Test Isn't What You Think

Abraham goes up a mountain with a theology of sovereign control. He is tested. He thinks he must prove His love for God. But really, this story is about God wanting to prove His sovereign love for Abraham.

Again, it can't be emphasized enough, "*we love because He first loved.*"[11] That's New Testament, but it's always been that way.

There are two theologies through which to interpret God's testing - sovereign control, or sovereign love.

If this story is interpreted through sovereign control, the conclusion is - God tests us to determine if our faith is worthy of His promise. Can we be trusted?

If this story is interpreted through sovereign love, the conclusion is – God tests us so we can be set free to live confidently sure that He is faithful with all He has promised. He can be trusted!

Every test by God is an invitation to transition from one narrative to another, from control to love, from orphan to son or daughter, from bondage to freedom, from fractured thinking to wholeness, from our perspective to His, from our best thoughts about who He is, to the truth about who He is, from our story, to the whole story; the one He is telling.

How we experience testing matters! If we think the test is about earning the promises of God, we will continually miss the point of the test. This will lead us to develop the heart of a prodigal or a religious Pharisee.

---

[11]*See 1 John 4:19*

But if we realize every test is an invitation, through faith, into a greater revelation of His always good love, we will navigate from bondage to freedom, we will be transformed, we will know righteousness, peace and joy regardless of the circumstances.

When God asks us to trust and obey Him in an area where we are insecure, it's so He can make us sure in the perfection of His love for us. Testing is the invitation to see God more fully, and be set free from fear.

In each test is available to us breakthrough for our thinking, for our future experiences and for the generations that follow us. This breakthrough is available to the extent that we, like Abraham, go into the test contending for resurrection life, contending for the goodness of God, the sovereignty of love.

We don't know what we don't know. And testing is the invitation to discover.

His Name was Will Hunting

The kid had been through the foster care system. He had been beaten and unloved. He had experienced the violence of the control narrative and had lost his ability to trust.

We talked about his past in one of our last sessions; about the abuse he experienced. It was a vulnerable moment for him, a scary but beautiful opportunity for me to be faithful with his trust; to expose the broken thinking that kept him bound to his past.

"Hey, Will, I don't know a lot. But you see this?" I lifted up the file that contained the history of his heartbreaking childhood, "All this? … It's not your fault.

"Yeah I know." He responded.

"Look at me, son. It's not your fault."

"I know."

"No, no you don't. It's not your fault…"

I spoke the truth to him over, and over, and over breaking through his pain. I spoke it over him until the revelation became his. He broke down and wept in my arms. The truth setting him free.

We don't know what we don't know. But oh, the wonder and grace when we discover the transformative revelation of sovereign love.

Freedom

Sometimes, we are so constrained by a lie we believe about God; sometimes it is so a part of our every thought, a foundational part of our existence, that it requires a radical act of trust to encounter the truth.

When a lie about the nature of God is so ingrained, there is only one way to be set free. We accept God's invitation to follow Him into the very heart of our broken perspective so the deception can be exposed. How is it exposed? Through a greater revelation of His good sovereign love in the very area that we were deceived, in the very lie that has enslaved us.

In these moments, we are able to see the perfection of His love, that the whole story is better than we thought, and we are set free.

Sometimes it looks like Abraham following God up a mountain so he can be set free from the perverse idea he lived in bondage to regarding worship and devotion.

Sometimes it looks like Peter following Jesus into a garden so he can face the ugly lie he clung to regarding establishing God's kingdom through an act of desperation.

These testing moments, these siftings in which Jesus prays for our faith, are always about us coming into greater freedom.

The lie that has defined our life, the lie that has often led to living in fear and desperation and insecurity, the lie that has left us unsure, striving, angry, broken and lost even when we are found, it's the lie of sovereign control.

And the enemy will use it to sift us, He will use it to attempt to separate us from complete trust, intimacy, truth and freedom. But God is love, His love is always good. And we are continually invited into opportunities to grow sure.

Generational Freedom

Abraham's testing was not just about his promise and freedom. It was about his descendants, us.

Abraham was to be the father of many nations. Being a father of many nations wasn't just about his progeny; it was about his revelation.

God has always desired that we live free of an appeasement based relationship with Him. But if Abraham didn't get revelation, he would have passed along his bondage to the next generation.

When Abraham was set free, so were his descendants. His breakthrough is our breakthrough, his revelation is our revelation.

It's the same with us. We *must* follow God into greater revelation, we *must* develop a theology of love, not just for our sakes, but for the sake of our kids!

How Do You Like Them Apples?

"You think you know something because you read it in a book? It requires living it. You don't know what you don't know."

Sean Maguire - Robin Williams character from the movie
Good Will Hunting

Faith works like this. We believe and then we see.

When we are tested, it's always about what we believe. Faith will always lead to a greater revelation of His good love.

If we look at the story of Abraham through the lens of sovereign control, we will come to the conclusion that God was testing Abraham to see if he was worthy of receiving such an amazing promise.

But if we read this story through the lens of sovereign love, we will come to the conclusion that God's testing was an invitation into a faith that would reveal the perfection of God's nature so Abraham could live free and have full access to the promises of God.

Our freedom, and our promises, are only available to us to the extent our theology transitions from control to love, to the extent that our narrative is transformed.

This wasn't a story of control, where God needed to know Abraham loved Him more than anyone else. That suggests God is needy. This wasn't a story of control where God needed to know Abraham would obey before God would follow through on His promises. That suggests God is petty.

This was a story about Abraham being set free from the horrific bondage of sovereign control so he could walk in the fullness of his promise. God was transforming Abrahams narrative.

He is always setting us free so we might fully discover all He has promised!

How do you like them apples?

chapter thirteen

FREE TO CHOOSE

I Didn't Like My Book Title...

I'm drawn to book titles that are generous and encouraging. I like titles that subtly invite the reader in, titles that suggest; nuanced emotive titles that inspire.

The title of this book is none of those things. It is like a meat cleaver, ham fisted and abrupt. There is nothing suggestive, no nuance, no subtlety. As to engendering an emotional response? Yeah, it does that. But it's likely not the inspired warming of a heart.

I imagine it's more in line with the response Jesus received when He told a crowd that if they desired to enter the Kingdom of heaven they would have to eat His flesh and drink His blood.[1]

Tension, confusion, frustration, disgust and even anger, those are some of the emotions I would guess this book title arouses.

---

[1]*See John 6:56,* NIV

Two Trees...

There were two trees in the Garden of Eden, *the tree of the knowledge of good and evil*, and the *tree of life.*[2]

Each tree represented a theology, a story. Control or Love. And Adam and Eve were free to choose.

These two narratives are still what define life on the planet. These two theologies still represent the two choices to be made. They are still the two stories being told today…

One

Jesus revealed sovereign love in everything He said and did, but I think the clearest revelation is discovered in His relationship with His Father and Holy Spirit.

When I look at their relationship, I see perfect love displayed in covenant surrender. I see trust and intimacy. I see righteousness, peace and joy.

Three persons, three wills, three personalities, and in everything, they are one. There is never a quarrel regarding roles, never a struggle for power, never a clash of wills. In all things, they are perfectly one.

How is this possible?

I would like to suggest it's possible for one reason, God is perfectly in control… but it's not the control we are so often shackled with.

I Didn't Like My Book Title...

It's not like I didn't try to find a different title. I did.

And I had plenty of suggestions too.

Believe it or not, there were other people who didn't seem to like my title either.

---

[2]*Genesis 2:7*

I had more 'seeker sensitive' ideas presented to me than there are names for seeker sensitive churches; wonderfully nuanced and suggestive titles that would ease the tension and make one feel comfortable.

I liked a good many of the suggestions too, except…

Well, if you have read thus far, then you know the problem; there is nothing 'seeker sensitive,' easy, or comfortable about the premise of this book. By now you also know that the title doesn't represent a bait and switch. It's not clever word play.

When Jesus said, *"Whoever eats my flesh and drinks my blood remains in me, and I in them"*[1] it wasn't bait and switch or clever word play, it was greater revelation. It was the whole story. The truth that would set us free.

It is my hope that this book is pregnant with that tension…

Two Trees…

There were two trees in the Garden of Eden. They represented the freedom to choose.

Adam was free. He could choose, control or Love. Adam chose *the knowledge of good and evil* and with it, bondage to a control narrative. He compromised his freedom. And yours, and mine…

In the narrative of control, the idea of *the knowledge of good and evil* not only seems good, it is a necessity. In the context of control, navigating life without a clear understanding of good and evil is not only dangerous, it is incredibly unsettling.

Early in their history, the Israelites were so incredibly unsettled by the control narrative that God obliged them with ten clearly written down rules so they could delineate *good* from *evil.*

But these ten commandments,[3] they would have seemed like a foreign language to Adam and Eve before the fall.

---

[1]*John 6:56*, NIV
[3]*See Exodus 20:1-17*

Before the fall, Adam and Eve were without sin. They knew nothing about *evil.* More to the point, they didn't need to. They were perfect in love. They had no internal wrestling match with sin. They knew nothing about shame, condemnation and death. They had never experienced sorrow, disappointment or sickness. They had no grid for evil and all his friends.

And *good*? To quote God, *"it was very good."*[4] Good was the very foundation of their existence, it was the air they breathed. Everything was very good because everything was perfect in love.

The fact is, before the fall, Adam and Eve navigated life without *the knowledge of good and evil* and it was stunning. They were infinitely free and daily growing in love and intimacy with God and each other.

Can you imagine the heart rending devastation both they and God experienced when they realized that they had sold their freedom for the knowledge of evil?

Not My Will, But Yours Be Done

"Father, if you are willing, take this cup from me; yet not my will, but yours be done."[5]

Jesus was in the Garden of Gethsemane when He prayed this. He was in such emotional anguish that He sweat drops of blood. He knew He was about to experience the greatest horror of His life. He was headed to a cross where He would feel the heartbreaking sense of separation that comes with the sin of this world.

Jesus told us He only did what He saw His Father do[6] and only said what He heard His Father say.[7] Jesus didn't take a breath without the wonder of His Father's presence. He didn't make a move without the infilling power of the Holy Spirit.

Every thought, every experience, every heartbeat was a display of covenant surrender – the Father, Son and Holy Spirit walking the planet as One. Jesus lived every second immersed in the lavish revelation of

[4]*Genesis 1:31,* NIV
[5]*Luke 22:42,* NIV
[6]*See John 5:19*
[7]*See John 12:49*

perfect love – sure in His Father, confident in the Holy Spirit.

That didn't change in the garden. Jesus was no less in His Father and no less filled with Holy Spirit when He prayed, *"Not my will, bit yours be done."*

My point? If we interpret this interaction between Jesus and His Father through the narrative of control, we might conclude that somehow, just this once, there was a wrestling match within the Godhead. As though God the Father was demanding God the Son to bow to His will. But that's just not true!

When Jesus, only saying what He heard His Father say, prayed, *"Father, if you are willing, take this cup from me,"* He was echoing His Fathers breaking heart.

And when Jesus, filled with Holy Spirit, said, *"Not my will, but yours be done,"* the Father and Holy Spirit were saying it right back to Him.

Please get this, Jesus' prayer wasn't revealing some battle of wills; this was not a Son capitulating to the demands of a Father. This was covenant surrender; three powerfully free individuals revealing what it is to be perfectly yielded to one another in the greatest circumstantial tension of history.

And in this surrendered agreement, Jesus went to the cross on behalf of the Trinity.

Jesus, perfectly in control...of Himself – in covenant surrender, chose to lay down His life.

The Father and Holy Spirit, perfectly in control...of Themselves – in covenant surrender, for the sake of the world, chose to give Jesus even unto death.

Love, sacrificial sovereign Love, for the joy set before Him, free and in full control of Himself, chose to endure the cross, scorning its shame. And He forever destroyed the bondage of sovereign control so we could be free.

I Didn't Like My Book Title...

It felt formulaic and I don't paint with that brush…

And what if the title caused people to want to debate in order to prove me wrong. That's the last thing I want to do with my time. To me, debating to prove something is often an act of futility; a finite interaction mostly focused on *the knowledge of good and evil* instead of an impartation of *everlasting life…*

My great hope for this book is not to prove, but reveal. The phrase, "I would like to suggest" is one of my favorite ways to reveal. This book title doesn't suggest, it positions the reader in tension before they even start reading it…

Two Trees...

When Jesus lived, died and rose, it most certainly wasn't to give us more knowledge regarding good and evil; He was redeeming our narrative. He came so that we *"may have life, and have it to the full."*[8]

Jesus is Life. Resurrection life.[9]

Jesus, through His resurrection, restored access to the infinite freedom Adam and Eva once reveled in.

There are two trees in our garden, and once again, we are free to choose. We can choose to live in the bondage of *the knowledge of good and evil* or we can choose to live in the freedom and power of *resurrection life.*

Self-Control

In the Garden of Eden, the first Adam enslaved all humanity to the narrative of control. In the Garden of Gethsemane, Jesus, the second Adam, chose sacrificial love and redeemed our narrative.

Then He sent us Holy Spirit so we can control ourselves, so we can know the same freedom.

---

[8] *John 10:10,* NIV
[9] *See John 11:25*

"But very truly I tell you, it is for your good that I am going away. Unless I go away, the Advocate (Holy Spirit) will not come to you; but if I go, I will send him to you."[10]

The same Holy Spirit that dwelled in Jesus throughout His life, that empowered Him through the cross, the same Holy Spirit that was with Him through death, that raised and seated Him at the right hand of the Father;[11] that same brilliant Holy Spirit is alive in us. And one of the evidences, one of the fruits of His in-filling presence is self-control.

"But the fruit of the Spirit is love, joy, peace, forbearance, kindness, goodness, faithfulness, gentleness and self-control..."[12]

In every room Jesus walked in to, He was the person with the most power and authority. I would like to suggest there was one reason for this. He was the person with the most self-control and therefore the most freedom.

In the Garden of Gethsemane Jesus revealed this self-control. Jesus, intimate with the Father, filled with Holy Spirit, and fully in control of Himself, chose to lay down His life. In trust and covenant surrender, He displayed the greatest act of freedom the world has ever seen. This freedom was so powerfully complete that not even death could take it from Him; He rose. He is alive!

Jesus revealed the whole story and it was not about a God in control of the earth and all who inhabit it, it was about a God in control of Himself.

It's such good news!

My Book Title? It's Growing on Me

I wrote faithfully into the tension of this title for years, always assuming at some point a new title would present itself.

Along the way I often prayed, *"Father, what do you think about this title?"* And I would sense His great pleasure as He always responded the same way.

---

[10] *John 16:7,* NIV
[11] *See Mark 16:19*
[12] *Galatians 5:22,* NIV

"I really like the way you describe me, son."

And so, I would lean into His love and embrace the tension.

As I wrote, I contended. Not *for* His good love but *from* it. I never once wrote to prove the goodness of God. That's settled. I wrote to reveal Him.

And in writing from the perfection of His love into the tension of this title, I grew in revelation. I experienced transformation and greater intimacy. As the deadline for the title drew near, I found I had developed an admiration for it. And by the time this book was ready for print, I determined to keep it.

Why? Because I learned firsthand that there is *Life* to be discovered in this tension.

Life. That is the whole point.

You see, at some point in everyone's story, the question of God, control, and His good love will come up. And I believe this title is an invitation to a better way of thinking.

This book title positions the reader in tension before they even read a word. And this tension presents the reader continually with a decision.

Because there are still two trees in our garden...

Two Trees...

The cross wasn't acquiescence to a control narrative; it was the destruction of a control narrative. It was the nail in the coffin of a fear-based reality. It was the end of a behavior focused relationship with God; it was the complete revelation of the fact that Love has all authority, is the most powerful force on the planet and never controls.

Why would God give us the Holy Spirit, and in Him access to self-control, if God was in control? The very idea that God is in control separates us from the freedom of self-control.

And self-control was His gift to us. An invitation to once again live powerfully free. "*For God gave us a spirit not of fear but of power and love and self-control.*"[13]

Self-control is the evidence we are free, free to fully receive love, and free to fully love.

A free person is a person living with self-control. A free person operates in the context of trusting surrender to sovereign love. A free person lives in the intimacy of oneness with the Father, the Son and Holy Spirit.

There are still two trees, two choices; God-control, or the wonder, freedom and life transforming, world changing power of self-control.

The Freedom to Choose

I asked Jesus into my heart when I was five. It was the first time I tried to give Him control. He came into my heart powerfully, but He didn't take control, He did something infinitely better, He sent Holy Spirit.

Over the years, as I grew in revelation, God became my Lord, my Comforter, my Provider, my Friend, my Father; and all along the way, in every discovery of His good nature, I would try to give Him control. But God is love and He would not take control; not only that, He didn't want it. His passion was that I would grow intimate with Holy Spirit and discover the freedom and the power of self-control.

The fact is, God has never been, nor will He ever be, interested in control. No, His passion is that we would receive the gift He paid such a high price to give. The freedom of self-control discovered when we are one with Him.

Jesus humbled Himself, was born of a virgin, grew into a man, lived as a revelation, died and rose as an invitation – all so we could be free! Free from sin and death, free from the theology of control, free to control ourselves, free to choose Life.

We have the power to control ourselves dwelling within us. We have

---

[13] *2 Timothy 1:7*, ESV

the power to live a Spirit filled, Spirit breathed life.

This life is full with tension. The evidence of control is everywhere. But there are still two trees in the garden - control or Love. And we have the power dwelling inside of us to choose!

We can choose to live overwhelmed by the *knowledge of good and evil* or overflowing in abundant *life.*

We can choose to live intimately one in the Father, Son and Holy Spirit; fully operating in the freedom of self-control.

We can choose to surrender, to lay our lives down so we might experience what it is to live in the power of resurrection life.

We can choose to live in the narrative that will transform us, our families and every area of influence.

We can choose greater revelation and intimacy as a way of life.

When we live from the narrative of sovereign love we are the freest people in the room, the freest people on the planet, empowered to love in the same transformative way Jesus loved.

It's passed time we stopped living like God was in control and started living like He has empowered us to control ourselves. God is not in control; we are. We are empowered by the Holy Spirit to live sure in love as expressions of His Kingdom come.

We are free to choose - control or Love.

I pray we choose love.

back cover quotes

1. Bill Johnson - 2011 - "Is Good Really In Control Of Everything?" https://www.youtube.com/watch?v=zB1BGhvCij4
2. Donald Miller - Twitter quote, May 6th 2015 https://twitter.com/donaldmiller/status/595970043915141121?lang=en
3. Todd White – 2014 - Dan Mohler & Todd White, "Sovereignty" Is God In Control Of Everything? https://www.youtube.com/watch?v=Cz7hjm0TnaI
4. Andrew Womack – Sovereignty of God – Article on Andrew Womack Ministries website. http://www.awmi.net/reading/teaching-articles/sovereignty_god/
5. Graham Cooke – From his book, Radical Permission 2: The Ascended Lifestyle

about the author

Jason Clark is a writer, speaker and lead communicator at A Family Story ministries. His mission is to encourage sons and daughters to grow sure in the love of an always-good heavenly Father. He and his wife, Karen, live in North Carolina with their three children.

For more information go to
www.jasonclarkis.com or www.afamilystory.org

about a family story

A Family Story is a relational community of creatives; family and friends. We do life together, we envision and express God's love through our gifting's and grace. We are a tribe of worshippers, dreamers, storytellers, and preachers; a family of dads and moms, brothers and sisters, daughters and sons, united by our singular passion – to know and reveal God's perfect love.

Our online home is www.afamilystory.org. This is where we share what God is revealing through the lives of family and friends. There are some amazing books, albums, films, messages, and articles on this site, resources that will greatly encourage you as you journey into our Father's always-good love.

PRONE TO LOVE

BY JASON CLARK

"Jason takes on some of the hard stuff, and does so with honesty and panache. Prone to Love is straightforward and disarming, a breath of fresh air!"

—BONNIE CHAVDA, Founder & Pastor of All Nations Church, & The Watch of the Lord

If you have been around Christian circles long enough, you have heard the phrase, "child of God." As believers, we use language like this all the time describing our relationship with the Father—but do we *really know what it means?*

What if we actually lived out of the relationship and reality we talked, preached, and sang about? Easy. *We would change the world.*

The roadblock preventing us from stepping into our identities as sons and daughters of God is *not* lack of discipline, resources, or creative ideas. We have all of this...

What's missing? To discover who you are, first, you must know who the Father is and what He's like.

AVAILABLE IN STORES, ONLINE AND AT
WWW.AFAMILYSTORY.ORG

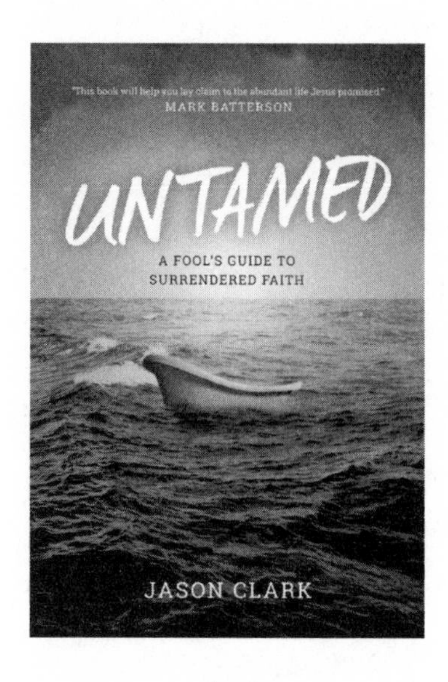

UNTAMED

BY JASON CLARK

"There is a difference between making a living and making a life. So many people settle for the former. God invites and calls us to the latter. I believe this book Jason has written will help you lay claim to the abundant life Jesus promised."

—MARK BATTERSON, *New York Times* Best-selling Author of *The Circle Maker*

You were made for *more.* Can you sense it?

There is a desire in every human heart to be part of something bigger and greater than themselves. We search in many different places, hoping we can fulfill this longing. We chase after careers, relationships, family, possessions, status, and addiction. Some pursuits are good, some are destructive—*none* of them can ultimately satisfy the cry of our hearts.

Get ready to start living Untamed and...

- Trade your life of striving for God's journey of abundance and adventure.
- Experience freedom to pursue radical dreams.
- Overcome your fears, take wild risks, and experience the impossible.
- Live out the promises God has placed within you.

You were created to dream...and dream *big.* Discover how to take the limits of your dreams and start experiencing the abundant life that you were made for!

AVAILABLE IN STORES, ONLINE AND AT
WWW.AFAMILYSTORY.ORG

FREE AS A LEELEE BIRD

BY AIMEE PERRY

"I thoroughly enjoyed reading this book to my 7 and 9-year-old kids! The story was moving and left us discussing forgiveness and the beauty and importance of this act of grace."

—B-ERB

Five-year-old Leelee is as free as a bird and full of joy. That is, until her best friend hurts her heart. Sad and confused, Leelee sleeps and finds in her dreams that her once free bird has become trapped in a cage of un-forgiveness. Teased and mocked by her captors, the great bird never gives up hope, believing that Leelee, her hero and her heart, will be brave enough to forgive her friend and free her once again. Will Leelee find the courage to forgive?

SAGE THE TREASURE HUNTER

BY AIMEE PERRY

"The whimsical illustrations and beautiful flow of writing held my 5-year-olds attention as the powerful truth of its message invaded his heart. Good, good stuff!"

—LIZA

For 8-year-old Sage who lives by the sea, nothing compares to finding lost treasure in the sand! An old trinket here, a shiny ring there, each day brings new surprises for Sage, and Sage alone! One day, Sage arrives to find others digging on her beach! What if they steal her treasures? This cannot be! Angered, Sage turns to leave and collides with a kindly old woman who teaches her how precious she is, and that real treasure is found within.

AVAILABLE IN STORES, ONLINE AND AT
WWW.AIMEEPERRY.COM & WWW.AFAMILYSTORY.ORG

JACK STAPLES

BY JOEL N. CLARK

JACK STAPLES - Eleven-year-old Jack's ordinary life is upended when mysterious creatures attack his hometown and he is whisked into a fantastical adventure filled with danger at every turn...

This is a wild ride that is best started early in the evening and with hot tea mixed with honey. Early because your kids will not let you stop with just one chapter and hot tea with honey for your voice because they won't let you stop after the second, third and fourth either. "Please dad, one more chapter" and "It's still early" will be phrases you become very familiar with as Clark and Batterson are experts at the cliff hanger. From the first page to the last, these books will fascinate and expand the imagination - enjoy